ENDORSEMENTS

Elle has discovered how to "Dwell" in the Secret Place of the Most High God and has learned what it means to "Abide " under the Shadow of The Almighty! Trekking through the muddy waters of pain and degradation, while embracing heart-ache after heart-ache, to arise as a "sweet smelling aroma" to our God, is not only a lesson in perseverance, but a testament of God's ever-loving Grace; Elle unpacks this masterfully! *Bridal Redemption* captivates your attention and massages your heartbeat, while purposefully revealing the true "Power of the Cross"—Well Done "Elle"! Great Book...Great Read... Great Author!

Pastor D Robinson
Network Director of Pastoral Care
Trinity Broadcasting Family of Networks

Elle is a great writer...and conveyed her personal story and her love for the Lord very well as well as His love for us. *Bridal Redemption* is very balanced...very personal, very Bible-focused and very Jesus-oriented. I loved that. Elle did a wonderful job sharing her heartfelt pain, sorrow and shame and God's rich mercy, forgiveness and love. Well done!!

Beth Jones
Co-Lead Pastor, Valley Family Church, Kalamazoo, MI
Author of *Getting a Grip on the Basics Series*

I have known my best friend, Elle, for the past 11 years. I have walked with her and watched her believe, stand, and live out knowing, "God is good." Through the trials of suffering, loss, and shame, she has literally lived out of that secret place with her Redeemer, through every place in her being, knowing that He is good. *Bridal Redemption* will take you on a journey of true life experience, that allows you to know and see the greatness of our God. All of His promises never let go of us and He is wonderfully God! Thankful and proud of Elle!

Kate McGovern
Life Purpose Leadership Coach
Real Life Restores

Bridal Redemption

Bridal REDEMPTION

Heal Your Past and Live Victoriously Through the Intimacy of Christ's Love

Elle Stahlhut Roetzel

Bridal Redemption,
Heal Your Past and Live Victoriously through the Intimacy of Christ's Love

Copyright © 2016 Elle Stahlhut Roetzel
All Rights Reserved

Cover Design by LSD

ISBN 978-1-943526-85-7
Library of Congress Control Number: 2016914479
Author Academy Elite, Powell, OH

Published by Author Academy Elite,
P.O. Box 43, Powell, OH 43035
www.AuthorAcademyElite.com

DEDICATION

This book is dedicated to the One who has loved me before I was loveable and has always seen me through the finished work of His cross—Jesus Christ, my Lord and Savior. He is my Bridegroom who calls me into the intimacy of His love and provides me with all that I will ever need or desire. Without Jesus loving me so deeply, pouring His grace and love out upon me, and drawing me into the intimacy of His love, I would never have been healed and experienced victory through the storms of my life. This is for Him, the Lover of my soul.

CONTENTS

Section 3: The Bridal Chamber

Shulammite Bride to her Bridegroom:

"My beloved is mine and I am his…."

Song of Songs 2:16

FOREWORD

Healing. Victory. Peace. Are these possible in the world today? Elle Stahlhut Roetzel not only believes that they are but also shows through the backdrop of her story that it's possible to live out these truths through an intimate relationship with Jesus Christ, our Bridegroom.

Everything has been made available to us through the cross of Christ. Elle shares the keys necessary to access and apply these truths in our lives. We can live the victory that is ours through the storms—untouched, unmoved, and stronger on the other side.

Elle shares her past, the life she kept hidden for many years. She discovered that keeping the past buried doesn't make it go away. When it springs up, it can spiral us into a deep dark pit and keep us from hearing the voice of truth that heals and sets us free.

As she shares her story of healing, you will be encouraged and strengthened to grab hold of your own healing. You will walk with her as she reveals the healing love of Jesus that set her free.

Elle's candid truth about the trials she has walked through and the keys that she has discovered by walking closely with Jesus reveals how to walk in victory no matter the circumstances or storms that come.

The analogy of the Jewish wedding customs brings a deeper revelation of how the Bride is to walk in victory with her Bridegroom. Christ, our Bridegroom, is committed to us and will never leave us or forsake us. This gives us strength and peace to face our past and receive His healing.

As a Bride waits and prepares herself for her Bridegroom to come for her on their wedding day, we are to prepare our heart and be transformed by the renewing of our mind. Preparation is a time of replacing the lies that we have agreed with and exchanging them for God's truth.

This is no longer simply a knowledge of the truth. Through the storms, it becomes our experience of the truth. Elle shares this revelation by integrating her story with the truth of God's Word.

PROLOGUE

The time of waiting was over. She would not be alone now. She would never be alone again.

The months of preparation leading up to this day had taken so much out of her. She had known that the Bridegroom was hers—He had committed Himself to her—but it was still a time of learning. There were days full of exhilaration, but there were also days when she had struggled to put one foot in front of the other.

There was a time when she had questioned the depth of His love, a time when she had made terrible choices with the most agonizing consequences. She had known of Him, but she had not known Him. That was the difference. She thought back to the decisions she had made and the things that she had put first in her heart, before her Bridegroom. Oh, the heartache! She had wanted control. She had wanted fun and freedom. If she had only known the miseries to come.

Remembering the past, but no longer feeling the pain, caused her to fall deeper in love with the One who was taking her home.

The day she learned of her pregnancy. The day she decided to end it. The day she realized what she had done.

How could she have killed her own baby? She had dreamed of being a mother since she was a little girl. And now there was nothing she could do. She had been unable to silence the voices in her head. They tormented her for 19 years.

She had carried on, struggling against shame and guilt, unaware that she could receive love and healing from her Bridegroom. She had finally come to the end of herself. As she looked over at Him now, she was so thankful for His patience with her. He had never given up on her.

The day that He showed how He had never left her. The day He redeemed everything for her. The day He brought pure joy into her heart.

That healing was only the beginning of her preparation. Illness, death, fear, and loneliness had since assaulted her battle-weary heart, but she had chosen the truth of His love for her.

The day she heard the diagnosis. The day she believed for healing. The day her world came crashing down.

But there was her Bridegroom, right there beside her— bringing her peace in the place that could never bring peace and giving her strength when she wanted to crumble. He had come for her at that moment. She had heard the shout. He wasn't going to leave her there. He had prepared a place for them to be together.

She was ready to enter into the most intimate place with Him. With her heart beating in anticipation, she could see that they were nearing the bridal chamber. She heard the sound of celebration in the distance. She would now be taken into the most intimate of places. She would be able to look into the depth of His eyes and know that He had carried it all. He had poured Himself out so that she could be here with Him.

This woman is me. This is my story of the Bridegroom's redeeming love for His Bride.

INTRODUCTION

We are the Bride of Christ. What does that mean? How are we to live with Jesus Christ as our Bridegroom? This is something that I have wanted to understand in a deeper way for years. I wanted to walk so deeply in Him that nothing else in this world would matter. I wanted my heart to beat more loudly and quickly at just the thought of Jesus.

My passion for this intimate relationship did not begin when I first accepted Christ as my Savior. I was raised in a Christian home and loved reading the Word of God at a very early age. I accepted Christ as a little girl and considered myself a Christian though I didn't understand the relationship that Christ died to give to me.

It wasn't until my world began falling apart that I started reading the Word of God again, recommitted my life to the Lord, and allowed Him to begin transforming me. His Word came alive to me. It spoke to my heart, and I hungered for the fullness of what I read in the Word.

I would read about overcoming in my life, and yet on a daily basis, I wasn't overcoming.

It was through my hunger for more that I discovered that my inability to live out that fullness was because of the scars and soul attachments that I had agreed to when I was walking down my own path in life. Though I had recommitted my life to Christ and turned from soulish living, I still had attachments that kept me bound. The strongholds in my soul (my mind, will, and emotions) kept me from believing and living out the truths that I desired in my life.

But how do we begin to live with Him this way, as we walk with our physical body through this world and its pain, disappointments, frustrations, hurts, and storms?

The Song of Songs is a poem describing the relationship of two lovers and their deep love for each other. This book of the Bible is also referring to Christ's love for you, His Bride, and how you are to love and seek after Him as your Bridegroom.

"Behold, how beautiful you are, my darling, Behold, how beautiful you are! Your eyes are dove's eyes" (Song of Solomon 1:15).

This is the Bridegroom speaking of His Bride. A dove looks steadily at its mate, never distracted or moved.

Christ is declaring over us, His Bride, that our eyes look only to Him, steady and unwavering, seeing no one besides Him. In the midst of our storm or the joy of life overflowing, He is the one who has our complete heart and our attention.

As we look steadily on Him as the One who completes us, the One who loves us, we receive that love. We, in turn, fall more and more in love with Him. In the storms of life, we hear nothing but His voice. No matter what else the world offers us, we desire only Him. He is the only One who completes us. He is the only One whom we trust, lean on, and desire with a heart that is undivided.

This sounds beautiful. Is it possible? Is it possible to walk through this world and live out of the depths of His love for us so that the storms of life leave us unmoved, stronger than when we entered them?

He has provided everything for us on the cross, everything for life and godliness. He gives us this picture of love, because not only is it the longing of our heart, it is the longing of His heart for us. He is the One who has pledged Himself to us. He loved us first with a love that has no bounds. He put our longing into words and painted a picture for us. The cross completes this picture of His love and our relationship with Him and in Him.

In this book, I share my experience of Jesus through the storms and difficulties of my life, and how His love and truth enabled me to discover that we can live from a place in Him that allows us to be conquerors and overcomers in this life. We don't have to wait until Heaven to overcome.

The book you hold in your hands is also about redemption—Christ's redemption for us at the cross. Why would I want to put these two together? What does that mean for us as believers, His Bride?

God is a Redeemer. "Redeem" means "to buy back." He can redeem our messes. His sacrifice was greater than my messes. He is such an awesome God, full of mercy and grace. Because I am His, He doesn't see me through my mistakes. He sees me through what He has already done.

When we become Christ's very own, we don't come to Him pure and clean. He is the One who cleanses us from all unrighteousness. He purifies us by His blood and the washing of His Word. So, to be His Bride walking fully in all that He has for us, we need to experience His redemption in every area of our life and receive healing in the pain and brokenness in our souls.

As you journey with me, you will discover the keys to finding healing for your past and receiving the depth of the Lord's love for you. This is yours no matter where you have walked, no matter what you have done. Victory in your present circumstances can be yours—is yours—as you receive all Christ has for you and as you walk in unity and agreement with Him.

This is the Bride, fully redeemed from her past, swept away by His love for her, able to walk in victory through everything and awakened into all that He has died to give her. Can you feel it? Can you sense what lies before you? I am so excited for you to discover Jesus as your everything, and for you to arise as the redeemed Bride into your destiny.

The format for this book includes excerpts from my personal journaling with the Lord. He is no respecter of persons. What He has done for me He will do for you.

I also have a section of application questions to help you reflect on and experience God's truth in your life and your current circumstances. Freedom awaits you. Victory awaits you. Your destiny is right before you. Your Bridegroom is calling.

SECTION 1
The Betrothal

A betrothal was the legal side of marriage for the Jewish people. It was a covenant for them, called a *kiddushin*. Commonly, it was done by the payment of a bride price in the presence of two witnesses and reciting the marriage formula, "Thou art consecrated to me according to the law of Moses and of Israel." From that time on, the woman was reserved for the man until the day of the wedding ceremony. This was a binding commitment to each other like our modern-day wedding ceremony.

You and I are betrothed to Jesus. When we are wooed by His love for us and when we receive Him as our Lord and Savior, we become His. We have access to everything that Jesus did for us on the cross. We have become a new creation in Him (2 Corinthians 5:17). He has committed to us, and we are now committed to Him.

If you have never asked Christ to be Lord and Savior of your life, please see Appendix A for Scripture and more information.

When we receive salvation, it is the spirit part of us that is made new. Our soul (which is our mind, will, and emotions) is not made new because that is the part of us that gets transformed as we continue to walk with Christ. This is where all the hurts and pains and soul attachments reside. So many new Christians "white-knuckle" a changed and transformed life. By this, I mean that they try and try as hard as they can to live as a believer in Christ is supposed to live. Our outer life flows out of our inner life. After salvation, if we attempt to live an outer life with no changed inner life (our soul), then we are setting ourselves up for failure. We will fall into condemnation, guilt, and eventually shame, then jump right back on that hamster wheel, attempting to white-knuckle it again. Many new believers would rather give up and walk away.

Romans 12:1–2 states, "Therefore I urge you, brothers and sisters, by the mercies of God, to present your bodies [dedicating all of yourselves, set apart] as a living sacrifice, holy and well-pleasing to God, *which is* your rational (logical, intelligent) act of worship. And do not be conformed to this world [any longer with its superficial values and customs], but be transformed *and* progressively changed [as you mature spiritually] by the renewing of your mind [focusing on godly values and ethical attitudes], so that you may prove [for yourselves] what the will of God is, that which is good and acceptable and perfect [in His plan and purpose for you]."

How do we renew our mind? By placing the Word of God in us and not conforming to worldly attitudes and standards.

Hebrews 4:12–13 says, "The Word is alive and full of power [making it active, operative, energizing, and effective]; it is sharper than any two-edged sword, penetrating to the dividing line of the breath of life [soul] and [the immortal] spirit, and of joints and marrow [of the deepest parts of our nature], exposing and sifting and analyzing and judging the very thoughts and purposes of the heart."

Katie Souza in her book, *Soul Decrees[1]*, states, "God's Word is so sharp it can divide soul from spirit. What does that mean for you? Many issues people deal with are coming from their souls, but most never know it—so they don't take action that could set them free. How many times have you cried out to God, 'Why is this happening to me?' Well, as you decree His Word over your life, its 'active and effective power' will slice through the confusion, get right to the wound that is deep in your soul, and heal it."

I always wondered why, if I was a new creation, I acted the way I did. I would become deeply hurt so quickly, just because of something somebody might say. Those words touched old wounds and took me to the depth of pain that was attached to my prior experiences. The wound caused me to have wrong thinking, wrong doing, and wrong feelings. I needed to act on, believe, and declare the Word that was in me in order to heal me and break the strongholds that were keeping me from living all that Christ had died to give me.

"...receive and welcome the Word which implanted and rooted [in your hearts] contains the power to save your souls" (James 1:21).

Soul Decrees[2] states, "The word 'saves' means to 'to save one suffering from disease, to make well, heal, restore to health.' The Word of God has the supernatural ability to heal our bodies as well as every wrong thought, free our will from bondage and cause us to experience healthy, God-given emotions."

As a believer, Christ is betrothed to you. Even if your life doesn't look pretty or you are not living in the fullness of life, He is committed to you. He is not going to walk away because you have "failed" as a Christian. He isn't going to see you as inferior because you are struggling to live how He has called you to live. You are His. His blood has abolished sin by His sacrifice once and for all (Hebrews 9:21–28). Our sins and our lawbreaking He will remember no more, for there has been an absolute forgiveness and cancellation of the penalty of our sins and no more sacrifice is required (Hebrews 10:17–18).

CHAPTER 1

Healing Our Past

When the news hits, not *if*, we can be carried away by our emotions. Pain from our past brings instability into our storm making it difficult for us to know who Jesus is and that He is for us **in** the circumstance.

The first step on the road to victory is being healed in our hearts from our past pain. That brokenness can keep us from hearing and believing the truth. In the midst of the whirlwind of voices and thoughts, this helps us to distinguish whose voice we will listen to. When our heart is healed, it is sealed off by Christ's blood from the enemy's whispers.

What we believe in our heart determines whose voice will become the loudest—our Savior's voice or our accuser's—and the one we will choose to listen to will determine our path.

The first time I experienced words coming out of nowhere and having the power to take me to my knees happened in 1999. Back then there was a chasm in my heart that agreed with the lies spoken. The pain was buried very deep, and Satan waited very patiently for just the right moment to remind me of what I had done. Back then, I didn't know that these words, which sounded like my own thoughts, could be spoken from the enemy of my soul. The pain in my heart knew that I didn't deserve any better. The pain in my heart didn't allow me to know that the Lover of our soul doesn't speak the kind of words that knock us to the ground until we're hardly able to breathe. Even when He is correcting us, His Words always come bathed in love and peace, and they lead us to Him.

The foundation for walking in victory in the storms is to receive healing in our heart for the wounds that still have a hold on us. We need to be healed in the places that keep us from knowing the truth of God's deep and passionate love.

It is important to know that when you go back for healing, you don't go alone, and you don't go to roll around in it. You take Jesus with you. You allow Him to shine a light on the place where pain and brokenness entered into your heart. When truth is shining a beacon of light on the brokenness, Satan can no longer drag you around by your nose. Strongholds in your thinking can no longer keep you out of truth and agreement with the Lord. You may know truth, but your heart is your "believer" and holds the expectation of what you will receive. (I have heard this called the "believer expector," and will use this term throughout the remainder of the book.) If your heart is broken, there has been agreement with the enemy in that place of pain. This means that you agreed with a lie. This is why healing is important. We must know the truth and believe the truth to experience victory.

> The foundation for walking in victory in the storms is to receive healing in our heart for the wounds that still have a hold on us.

If your heart is broken, the pain is still down there, and you won't have the power to decide when the hurt is going to come barreling to the surface. It might be years, as it was for me, or it could be every few months, but it will come out. It doesn't go away on its own. Satan knows exactly where and when to push the buttons, and as in my case, he knew exactly when to remind me of what I had done.

In 1999, my husband Ronnie and I had two sons and were happily expecting our third child. Unfortunately, the pregnancy ended in miscarriage. I was grieved, but at the same time, I was so thankful for how the Lord helped us through the miscarriage by surrounding us with friends, family, and a compassionate hospital staff. I was less than three months pregnant, but it doesn't really matter how far along you are; the loss of the dreams for your child are very real.

We had planned a trip to Disneyland which happened to fall one week after the miscarriage. We decided to continue with our plans because the boys would be disappointed if we canceled. As we walked around the park, it seemed that everywhere I looked there were pregnant women. I slowly became resentful of their bulging stomachs. By the end of our trip, I had full-blown anger raging in my heart.

"Why do they get to have their baby while mine died?" was the question swirling around inside my heart.

Upon our return from the trip, everyone's schedule went back to normal. My husband was working in another city, so he wasn't home, my older son was in elementary school, and my younger son slept late most mornings. As I walked into the bathroom, I heard the answer to the question I had been asking in my heart the week before. "You lost this baby because, years ago, you killed your first baby. This is your punishment. This is what you deserve."

I fell on the floor and attempted to cry, but all I could do was open my mouth and moan. The chasm that had just been opened up in my heart was massive, dark, and bottomless.

The guilt and the pain in my heart knew that I deserved to have this miscarriage. Why wouldn't I be punished for killing my baby?

I had never told anyone what I had done in 1981. My husband did not know, my family did not know, and my Christian friends did not know. It was something so dark and loathsome that I knew I could never tell anyone.

I suffered this pain from my "punishment" in silence. Everyone around me just thought that I was having a really hard time getting past the miscarriage. On a daily basis I would cry, falling into a depression. I fell into that deep dark pit that had no bottom, no place to land. I'm not sure how I was able to keep my emotional state from everyone else. I felt no hope and no comfort, even from my time with the Lord. To me, what I had done was so horrible I could not even talk to the Lord about it. I spent time with Him for hours every day, in His Word and praying, but because I was holding on to the lie, I was unable to hear His truth in the midst of my pain.

To survive, I stuffed the pain down so that I didn't have to feel the torment every day. After 18 years, I had become a master at hiding.

> Because I was holding on to the lie, I was unable to hear his truth in the midst of my pain.

The only prevailing thought was that, because of what I had done, I might never have another child. I might never be allowed to get pregnant again. This would be my ongoing punishment.

We eventually moved for my husband's job, and the excitement and planning that goes into building a house five hours away filled my time. I was able to fill my days with thoughts of our new home and life in another city rather than the loss of my child and the punishment that I was given. Many things had to be done, and my family depended on me. Again, I practiced shoving the pain down to deal with life.

After our move to our new home, I became pregnant again—this time with twins. This was the desire of my heart. We were so thrilled. After Christmas, I went to my first doctor's appointment. It was a cold January day, and the wind was blowing hard—not only in the natural, physical world but the spiritual realm as well. A storm was coming.

As a routine, they did an ultrasound. They could not find my babies. There were two sacks but no fetuses. The whirlwind began to toss me around as soon as I heard this news. My husband was not with me. It was a new doctor in a new city, and we hadn't known that there would be an ultrasound at the appointment. The doctors decided that maybe I was wrong about the date of my pregnancy, and so they gave me a nugget of hope that maybe I wasn't as far along as we had thought. I was sent home with the hope that my babies were all okay. I made an appointment to come back in a few weeks for another ultrasound to see the progress of my pregnancy.

I prayed and begged God to give me these children, to forgive me for what I had done, and show mercy on me. I was never able to talk directly with the Lord about "my punishment" and what "I deserved." It was too ugly to bring to His light and presence.

In the days of waiting for my next appointment, I clung to the hope that everything was going to be okay. I must have been off with my dates.

A few weeks later, Ronnie and I were told that our babies had not survived and that I would soon be miscarrying what remained of the pregnancy.

In the car with Ronnie, I was able to hold on to my emotions, which were boiling right under the surface. I waited until I could be alone in the house, in my bedroom, in my closet. My grip on the door handle of the car got tighter and tighter as the emotions raged inside of me. It was the only thing I could cling to, and I was holding on for dear life.

The chasm inside me was even bigger than the time before. I was shown no mercy for the pain because I didn't know there was mercy for me in the midst of it. I found myself in the closet in a fetal position almost every day. Then the miscarriage. It was horrible and included a day in the ER due to the hemorrhaging.

I was in horrible emotional pain after that. Again, nobody knew the source of my depression, but since this was a more traumatic miscarriage, they gave me grace for the way I was reacting. Every day I found myself curled up in the closet, swallowed up by the dark pit that called out to me. At night it was worse. The darkness of the night made everything worse. I would wake up in the middle of the night unable to go back to sleep. Hopelessness was getting a stronger and stronger grip on me. As I went to Bible study and interacted with my family and friends, they never would have guessed that I spent my days in a fetal position. I appeared to be a strong woman of faith. I spent many hours with the Lord while my son was at preschool. I also spent time in my dark closet in pain.

Finally, one morning as I sat at my kitchen table, I cried out to the Lord that I couldn't do this anymore.

He whispered to my heart, "You need to go back with Me to the day that you had your abortion. You need to take Me with you and know that I was there."

I was stunned when I felt Him telling me to do this. Was He really talking to me about my abortion? I never spoke the word *abortion* to Him. In my time with Him, I always referred to it as "the circumstance in 1981." Now He wanted me to go back in my heart and take Him along? I knew I couldn't exist the way I was living but was unsure if I could do what He was asking me to do.

I finally decided that doing as Jesus asked couldn't be any worse than what I felt each day. If I was going to do this with Him, the only place I could do it was in the unfinished portion of my basement in the back corner. It was dark there, and it felt like the most appropriate place to remember a deep dark secret.

As I sat on the cement floor staring at the unfinished walls, my thoughts went back to 1981. I relived every moment of my abortion. I held the Lord's hand but couldn't look up into His eyes. I mostly cringed and cowered knowing He saw everything that I had done. He had seen it already, but this was me being aware of Him. I hadn't given Him any opportunity to be a part of my decision on that dreadful day.

I finally looked at Him as I made that choice. I could no longer hide and pretend it didn't happen. I knew that if I was to move past this, I had to see Him there. I had to see Him at the moment my baby was gone. Oh the pain, the tears, the cries of my heart as we walked through it together.

He was so pure and holy, and I was so dirty.

He was peace and love, and I was a broken heap on the floor.

But as I pressed on, His love overcame my pain. His purity washed away my filth. It was the hardest thing I had ever done in my relationship with the Lord. I had to trust Him in this.

A Holy God was listening to His daughter as she walked through her abortion. How could He even be there with me? How could He look me in the eyes and love me?

He was showing me that He was always there with me, even though at the time of my abortion I had never asked Him to be there with me.

The power of the cross was there with me that day. I chose to turn to Him as I walked through it again. The power of His blood was there for me as I turned to Him for forgiveness. The power of His love was there to hold me and love me even when I felt so completely unworthy and unlovable. Only a God that loves me more than anything I have ever done could have walked through that day with me and still called me His own, called me His daughter, called me His Love.

At that moment, I may not have felt any different, but what took place in my soul was enormous. I finally knew that I was forgiven. I could no longer hide what I had done from Him. Hiding and attempting to forget hadn't been very effective anyway. To know that He loved me in the darkest place of my life was a feeling I had never known before. Of course, I still wasn't going to tell anyone about this because I didn't want anyone to know what I had done. It was enough that Jesus knew, and I could now talk to Him about it.

His truth destroyed the lie that my miscarriages were a punishment. His love for me showed me that He had paid the price for my decision, not the loss of my children through miscarriage. The door that I had opened to Satan in my life by having an abortion was being slammed shut by the truth of my Savior's redeeming love for me.

"For our sake He made Christ [virtually] to be sin Who knew no sin, so that in and through Him we might become [endued with, viewed as being in, and examples of] the righteousness of God [what we ought to be, approved and acceptable and in right relationship with Him, by His goodness]" (2 Corinthians 5:21 AMPC).

"Therefore, since we are justified (acquitted, declared righteous, and given a right standing with God) through faith, let us [grasp the fact that we] have [the peace of reconciliation to hold and to enjoy] peace with God through our Lord Jesus Christ (the Messiah, the Anointed One)" (Romans 5:1 AMPC).

"Therefore, [there is] now no condemnation (no adjudging guilty of wrong) for those who are in Christ Jesus, who live [and] walk not after the dictates of the flesh but after the dictates of the Spirit" (Romans 8:1AMPC).

There was another layer of healing for me after that day—a layer that most of us don't encounter because even though we're forgiven, we think we're supposed to feel inferior to others because of what we have done or what has been done to us. It's our cross to bear. It's the label that will never be removed. This is shame.

A few years after the Lord had walked with me through the healing of my brokenness from my abortion, we were living in another city and my new friend, Kate, invited me to her house for prayer. I was so excited because I knew that she sought the Lord in the same way I hungered for Him. As we prayed, she looked at me and said there was something that I had done, but I didn't want anyone to know about and that the spirit of shame had hold of me in this area. I looked at her and thought, "There is no way I'm going to tell you about what I've done." As she continued sharing from her heart, there was such a beautiful presence of the Lord that I couldn't keep myself any longer from confessing my abortion to another person.

She said I had a spirit of shame. I remember looking at her and wondering, "What is that?" Before that day, I had never heard of shame spoken in that way. I had heard people say, "Shame on you." I don't even know if I knew what that meant, it was just a saying. As Kate shared with me, I realized I had been living with the spirit of shame for years and never knew.

As I confessed my abortion to her, the Lord continued to hold me in His love. Kate then prayed over me and broke the power of shame off my life.

I knew something had happened at that moment. Though I didn't know what shame was, shame knew me quite well. To completely break the stronghold of shame on my life, Kate told me that I needed to tell my husband about my abortion.

Even though I knew she was right, I had no idea how I would go about it. I began praying for just the right moment to tell Ronnie.

God was so good and did provide the moment. I still had to step out in faith through the fear of what he would say. Ronnie's response was only love and compassion for what had happened in my life. I knew that the enemy had lost his foothold in my heart because I didn't feel condemned, only loved, and the Lord's presence of peace was with us.

Shame makes us feel inferior and keeps us in the cycle of guilt and condemnation. Shame says, "I was wrong," and keeps us out of deep relationships, because if I am vulnerable you will see there is something "wrong" with me. Conviction says, "What I did was wrong." Conviction comes from the Lord, and shame comes from the evil one.

Isaiah 54:4 (AMPC) states, "Fear not, for you shall not be ashamed; neither be confounded and depressed, for you shall not be put to shame. For you shall forget the shame of your youth, and you shall not [seriously] remember the reproach of your widowhood any more. For your Maker is your Husband—the Lord of hosts is His name—and the Holy One of Israel is your Redeemer; the God of the whole earth He is called."

The Lord's promise to us in Isaiah 54:4 is to remove the shame and dishonor from us so that we remember it no more. If we are rooted and grounded in shame, the curse and power of shame can be broken through the cross. The cross erased it from His memory. The Lord is our Redeemer. He took our shame on the cross and gave us glory. He wants us to live free from the shame of our experiences and the choices we have made. Knowing that He has freedom for you is the first step to receiving it.

I knew I had broken free from that spirit when a few months later a group of us were praying for a young woman contemplating an abortion. I stepped forward and said I would lead out the prayer for her because I had had an abortion. Not one woman looked at me with condemnation. I had always thought that if I told anyone, they would condemn me, look down on me, and not want anything to do with me. These Christian women didn't even bat an eyelash. Instead, they encouraged me to pray because I now had an anointing in this area.

I went home that day amazed that I did not feel inferior to all the other Christian women praying with me. I was free, free to believe that I was no worse or better than anyone else in God's eyes, and I didn't have to prove my worth to Him.

As we move forward in our walk with the Lord, one of the foundational keys is to be healed from the brokenness and shame of our past. That brokenness remains in our soul and affects how we respond to the Lord. Our present situation flows out of that place in our heart. We are unable to receive from Him and see Him in His truth outside of that brokenness.

Satan's whispers to my heart that my child's death was my punishment would have sounded completely different if my soul had been healed. I was unable to stand up to his accusations with the truth of Christ's love because I didn't know Christ's love and forgiveness for me in that place. I only knew a deep, dark pit of pain and guilt. When I made the decision for an abortion out of fear, I was walking right into Satan's plan of destruction for my life. When we do as he wants us to, he doesn't leave us alone afterward. He comes back and uses it against us over and over again in an attempt to destroy us and keep us out of our destiny in Christ.

I had become Christ's when I was a little girl. I was His. At the betrothal, there was a covenant made with no turning back. I remained Christ's even as a young woman who had walked where I should not have walked, agreed with whom I should not have agreed with, and was dirty, needing cleansing and healing. Even though Satan came and attempted to take me down by telling me who I was in the midst of my miscarriages, Jesus my Bridegroom came and reminded me of my true identity and to whom I belonged.

Journal Entry

2/25/02

Dear Jesus, several weeks ago You held me and walked me through the events that happened 21 years ago. You helped me through them so I didn't turn my face and run away, but You held me and told me You loved me, even then and even more now. May I know that I do not stand condemned before God, but as a forgiven child through the blood of Jesus Christ so that I know Satan can't use that to chain me up.

Application Questions

1. Have you experienced a painful situation in your past that left you with brokenness, condemnation, and guilt?
2. Do you know that you are forgiven by the blood of Jesus? How can you also release forgiveness to those who have hurt you?
3. What bad fruit has grown in your life through the seed that was planted in agreement in your past?
4. How has this bad fruit affected your ability to trust in the truth of God's Word?
5. Ask Jesus to sit with you in that place of hurt and pain. Invite His truth in. If there is forgiveness for you

to release to others, ask the Holy Spirit to help you forgive, and say a simple prayer releasing them from your unforgiveness into the Father's love.

6. As you sit with Jesus in the place of your pain, ask Him what truths He has for you to replace the seeds of lies in your heart.

7. Receive Jesus' presence; receive His blood which washes you clean. Though you may not feel different, by faith agree with the Word and Jesus that you are forgiven, and the lies in your heart have been replaced with His truth.

8. Connect with me online at www.ElleUnlimited.com for further healing truth and encouragement.

CHAPTER 2

Experiencing His Love

"Jesus loves me." These are words that easily roll off our tongues and it's a song that we sang growing up. When we hear the music, we sing it without even thinking.

These words are so much more than a children's Sunday school song. These words are powerful and cry out to be experienced, not just sung.

Ephesians 3:16–19 says, "May He grant you out of the riches of His glory, to be strengthened *and* spiritually energized with power through His Spirit in your inner self, [indwelling your innermost being and personality], so that Christ may dwell in your hearts through your faith. And may you, having been [deeply] rooted and [securely] grounded in love, be fully capable of comprehending with all the saints (God's people) the width and length and height and depth of His love [fully experiencing that amazing, endless love]; and *[that you may come] to know [practically, through personal experience] the love of Christ which far surpasses [mere] knowledge [without experience]* (emphasis mine), that you may be filled up [throughout your being] to all the fullness of God [so that you may have the richest experience of God's presence in your lives, completely filled and flooded with God Himself]."

Paul's prayer for us is that we not only come to know of Jesus' love for us but that we have a personal experience of His love. Jesus' love for us is not for our head to comprehend—it is for our heart to encounter.

What is the difference, you may ask?

Don't I need to know that He loves me?

Yes, you do need to know that He loves you. Knowing that He loves you is just the beginning. Once we know He loves us, we can pursue the love He has for us and fully expect an experience of it in our heart.

Your heart is your "believer expector." What you believe in your heart is what you expect out of your experiences. If your head is the only place where you "know" Jesus loves you, then it means that your heart has a completely different understanding and expectation. When we believe that God is good and that He loves us no matter what, we can stand expecting in our circumstances for the goodness of God to show up. On the other hand, if you are not sure of God's love for you or feel unworthy of His love for you when you walk through difficult circumstances, it will be difficult to believe and expect God's love and goodness. Without believing that He loves you, you are more susceptible to Satan's lies.

I had been visiting a friend for the weekend, and on the way to the airport to catch my flight I shared with her how the Lord loved her and came to heal her broken heart from her recent divorce. I shared from Isaiah 61 and encouraged her to read it in the coming weeks.

As I sat on the plane waiting to take off, I thought about my conversation with my friend. I realized that though my heart was healed from my broken past and from the pain of my abortion, I was missing that last piece. There was still a place in my heart that hurt when I thought about my abortion and the Lord loving me. Here I was telling my friend that this is who Jesus is, yet I had not experienced it for myself, not to the depth that the Word said was mine. At that moment, I decided that I was going to seek after the Lord for the experience of His healing love that He said was mine. I didn't think it was right for me to be telling others that it was theirs if I hadn't experienced it for myself.

Over the next days and coming weeks, I pressed in. I can only explain it as grabbing hold of the Lord's garment and not letting go. I knew that this deep love and "binding up of a broken heart" was mine, but I had no idea what it looked like or how I could experience it. I would rise early in the morning and sit in the sunroom, in the chair I always sat in, at the Lord's feet. I would search the Scriptures, and I would tell Him how my heart still hurt. I would declare out loud that this love and healing from Him was mine. I just wouldn't let go. I wasn't going to turn back, and I wasn't going to give up. Some mornings I felt like I was making headway, and some mornings I didn't hear or experience a thing. But I didn't give up.

In Mark 5 it speaks about the woman with the issue of blood. She was an outcast and was not allowed to be in public according to Jewish law. She heard about Jesus. She heard about what He had done for so many others. Faith began to rise within her. She knew that if she only touched His robe, she would be healed. She braved the crowds. She braved the ramifications of being "caught" out in public. Jesus was in her town that day. He was surrounded on all sides by the people. People were touching Him, pushing on Him. It was only when the woman with the issue of blood came and touched His robe that He felt power go out of Him. She had come, believing and pushing her way through to Him. The Amplified Bible says that she knew she

16

was instantly healed from the cause of her symptoms. It wasn't just a little relief—it was to the very root that she was healed.

Jesus turned and asked who touched Him. This amazes me because He was being touched by everyone. But it was the woman who knew that by touching Him in faith she would receive His power. This is what I wanted. This is what I came seeking every morning from Him. I knew He had healing for my heart. I knew that it was mine, and I wasn't going to let go until I had touched His robe, pulled on His robe, and received everything that He had for me. I didn't want to be the crowd of people surrounding Jesus, touching Jesus, rubbing up against Jesus, and nothing happened. I was determined to be the woman who touched Jesus and received all that she had been seeking.

I will never forget one Sunday morning, early before church, the day I was forever changed. It didn't start out different than any previous day as I came to sit with the Lord. I got up early, prepared my required cup of coffee, and went to sit in my chair in the sunroom. I opened up my Bible and began reading His Word. I also had my journal open, writing down my praises to Him as I read and worshiped. Then, just like the sun rising and beginning to shine above the tree line, I felt His love pouring into my heart. It felt as if my chest was going to burst. The knowledge of His love flooded every injured place in my heart. It was better than anything I had ever experienced before. The hurt was just gone—replaced by overflowing passion and love. I cried, I danced, I laughed. I remember getting up from my chair and standing with my arms spread out to receive everything He had for me. I knew that whatever I had done before would not stop Him from loving me completely. I knew that anything I was doing right now in my life could not stop Him from loving me, that there was nothing I could ever do that could stop Him from loving me completely, just the way I was.

That experience changed me forever. No one can take what I experienced away from me or tell me that it wasn't true or real. I know that Jesus loves me. How do I know? Freedom—freedom that comes from His love overwhelming me. I was set free from my bonds that day. What is even more glorious is that I didn't even know I was bound. That's the surprising truth about freedom: we don't realize we are held back until Jesus releases us. We are so familiar with how we see ourselves and our relationship with the Lord that it can be like putting on our favorite comfortable clothing. It feels good. We know how it fits. We know what we can do in it, and we feel complete comfort wearing it. We don't feel bound when we are wearing that familiar clothing. Neither do we understand our bondage when we live in the familiarity of how we see ourselves and how we see the Lord; until we are set free in His love.

The experience of His love would not have been possible without first experiencing His healing in my brokenness. Our brokenness keeps us from believing that it is possible for Him to love us in every area of our life. Once those places of brokenness heal, we can seek Him and the depth of His love that He has for us. My shame and guilt were continually making me feel inferior. My abortion kept me from thinking that He could love me completely. Once I experienced His healing in my heart, His truth in the midst of the lies that I had believed, I was ready to go to a deeper level with Him. I could press in and not turn back.

Knowing His love through a personal experience sets us on a firm foundation for whatever may come our way in the future. Persecution and difficulty will come. The storms and broken world come from Satan who wants to rob, kill, and destroy our future. Satan attempts to knock you off your feet and keep you from walking in victory by reminding you of your past and dragging you back into the pain and torment and shame. In the midst of difficulties and storms that come out of nowhere, if we don't know that Jesus loves us, then we leave ourselves open to the lies that Satan whispers to us. These thoughts make us feel alone and unloved, questioning where God is in the midst of this. They keep us from looking up to Jesus to find truth and peace, and instead keep our eyes smack dab on the value we place on ourselves and the situation.

It's a vicious cycle where the enemy of our soul keeps dragging us around and around in our pain. Only the depth of Jesus' love for you can break this cycle. Knowing in your heart the depth of His love will allow you to expect victory. It'll help you see the good things that are ahead. If we can't see it, then we can't walk in it.

When you know that Jesus loves you, you know that there is always something good coming your way. The thing that just happened to you isn't because God didn't love you. It didn't happen because there was something that you did in your past and God's absence is a punishment.

Instead, you should know that it is always going to be okay. Even though it doesn't look like it, things are going to work out. Your hands may be empty at the moment, and precious things could have been taken from them, but because of God's love for you, you won't be down and out. You are not going to go without. There is always more in store for you. Hope. That is what you have. Hope and expectation today and tomorrow.

Lamentations 3:20–23 states, "My soul *continually* remembers them and is bowed down within me. But this I call to mind, therefore I have hope. It is because of the LORD's loving kindnesses that we are not consumed, because His [tender] compassions never fail. They are new every morning; great *and* beyond measure is Your faithfulness."

Journal Entries

2/5/07

Much was taken from me, Father. I had chosen to believe a lie, but now I praise You that You are truth, and the truth has set me free. I am free from the bondage, free from the tangled web of Satan's lie. Your love, Jesus, has set me free.

2/6/07

Jesus, You have set me free. I love You and I love Your Word. I love studying Your Word, and I love hearing the Holy Spirit speak truth to my heart. The truth of who I am in Christ sets me free, and the lie of the evil one about my identity keeps me in bondage. I am free.

Application Questions

1. Is there a place in your heart that hurts? Is there an aching in your heart that you think will always be there? Do you see now that the Lord's love for you is more than enough to heal your heart?
2. How can you seek after His heart of love for you so that you can be set free by His overflowing love?
3. As you seek after Him, you may find that it will take diligence and stamina on your part to continue pursuing Him. Will the satisfaction of experiencing His love and freedom be greater than your willingness to stay in the familiar, in the comfort of knowing how to respond in your hurt?
4. How will your relationship with the Lord change now that you have connected with His love for you?
5. Connect with me online for further opportunities to pursue and respond to Jesus' love for you. www. ElleUnlimited.com

CHAPTER 3

Knowing His Heart

We are well on our way to building our foundation as His Bride with eyes only for Him. As our heart begins overflowing with His love for us, we can move on without hesitation to find our way into His presence on a daily basis. What does this look like for the Bride of Christ? How can we sit at His feet and be filled with Him and His love for us?

As the Bride, it is the desire of our heart to be in His presence, to live out of His presence. His Word is the life source that we partake of on a daily basis to receive everything that we need for the day that is ahead of us.

"'For My thoughts are not your thoughts, nor are your ways My ways,' declares the Lord. 'For as the heavens are higher than the earth, so are My ways higher than your ways. And My thoughts are higher than your thoughts'" (Isaiah 55:8–9).

The Lord's thoughts towards us and for us are far different than the thoughts we have. His ways for our day are far different than the ways that we use to strategize and control. To understand His heart for us, we must go to Him and dig up the treasures that are waiting just for us.

We have covenanted ourselves to Jesus. When we asked Him to be Lord and Savior of our lives, He came into our heart (spirit), and we were saved. Our spirit was made completely new and pure and holy. But while our spirit is complete and filled, whole and ready to go, the rest of us has to catch up and be transformed. This is where the pursuit of Jesus changes us.

We need to pursue Him as He pursues us, coming to know Him in the Word. The Word becomes alive; it brings life, not death and condemnation. Your spirit becomes awakened, agreeing with the Word, and your soul comes into agreement, too. Your heart begins to believe what He says, and you come to know who you are because you know who He is. As you read the Word, you can read it back to Him saying who He is and who you are, and a song may rise within you.

Not pursuing Him can leave you empty and wanting in your life as a Christian. Everything is available and already given to you, yet you can be living far short of that fullness. We find ourselves wanting something more. Not knowing what it is and not knowing that it is already ours, we end up looking for the desire of our heart in every place but where we will actually be fulfilled, completed.

You are who He says you are; you can do what He says you can do, but if you don't know it you will never attain it. Pursuing Him releases that truth into our heart, our soul. The experiences we walk through will shake anything that we hold on to that isn't the truth. And as we hold on to anything other than the truth, we will be shaken along with them. Knowing and believing His truth is the only foundation that will keep us from being knocked down, broken, overcome, and destroyed.

> You are who He says you are; you can do what He says you can do, but if you don't know it you will never attain it.

It is important that as we walk through the trials of this world, we don't mix His truth with a little of this and a little of that. I have found that even Christian songs can repeat earthly theologies rather than the Word. I have caught myself repeating a line from a song as truth. I once shared a line from a song with someone who needed comforting. As I heard myself speaking the words, I began to wonder if this was even what the Word of God had said. I searched out the Word and discovered that though the song sounded like it had truth in it, it was based upon man's theology of who God is. When we don't know the Word of God, it is very easy for us to hear things, even from other Christians and Christian songs, and take those words as truth.

When we mix the Word with man's opinion—man's experiences, which can create theology—we will not be victorious. It is a watered-down foundation that is not solid, and will cause us to sink in the midst of trials.

One of my favorite Scriptures is Psalm 34:8. It says, "O taste and see that the LORD [our God] is good; How blessed [fortunate, prosperous, and favored by God] is the man who takes refuge in Him."

In this verse, David shared with us that by tasting the Lord we know He is good. Tasting is more than hearing the Word of God; it denotes an experience of the Word.

As we experience Jesus in the Word, it develops a hunger for more within us. The Bride's daily search is to find Jesus in the Word, to look for the one she loves and find His heart for her in all that she experiences in her day. This is how the Bride strengthens and prepares for her day. This is the Bride filling her lamp with oil to be ready for her day.

How can we know the Lord's heart if we are not partaking of His manna for us each day? How can we truly know who we are unless we go to the source to find the truth?

When we are saved, we become part of another Kingdom. We are a new creation and not of this world anymore. How do we interact in this new realm? How do we respond to the trials and storms of this world as a new creation? Is there even a different way to respond than the way we are taught in this world? What does it feel like or look like to live out of a place of victory and power rather than attempting to attain victory?

These are questions that can only be answered by our guidebook, the Bible. As we partake of the Word of God, we begin to understand how we are to respond to sickness, how we are to respond to tragedy, death, loss, finances, betrayal, pain, our past, and our present situation. We understand who we are and the power and fullness of our spirit.

As I have been in the Word, I have learned to respond to situations differently than I had in the past. One situation I remember was when I was going with a friend to hear a visiting pastor who was anointed in healing. I was so excited to be with other believers and hear and experience what he had to share.

When we arrived, my friend and I were greeted by another friend. She welcomed each of us and then proceeded to take my friend by the hand and tell her that she just had to meet this visiting pastor. I stood there feeling rejection coming at me full force. The hurt that came at my heart was too big to take. Thoughts of why I wasn't asked to meet him too, bombarded my mind. In fact, my flesh wanted to scream, "What about me?" It took everything in me to not run out of there before the evening had even begun.

This was not the first time that I had felt overlooked by others. I hated how it made me feel and how that hurt would attach itself to all the other hurt from prior experiences.

This time was different, though. I may have felt the unworthiness and rejection come at me, but then I said in my heart, "Lord you have never overlooked me. You have never rejected me. I am accepted by You and loved by You. So even if man overlooks me and rejects me, You never will. I bless my friend and release her into Your love, and I receive Your love in the midst of my hurt right now."

I would never have thought to speak those words over myself if I hadn't been reading them in the Word each day. Each day I read how much Jesus loved me and how He never rejected me and how I was accepted in Him. So without even thinking about it, I began to speak His Words of truth.

I immediately felt free of the rejection. His truth ministered to my heart, and I didn't become offended at the friend for what she had done. I knew it was not intentional, even though the pain in my heart was real. My mind and heart were being transformed by His Word, and I was learning how to take my thoughts captive to Christ Jesus.

Years ago when I had become pregnant and I had to make a decision about having an abortion, I didn't even hear the whisper of the Lord leading me. I didn't think about asking Him what He thought about my situation. I wasn't giving His thoughts time each day. I wasn't putting the Word in me to change me and transform me. I was giving time to other voices instead. The voice of this world, the voice of my favorite soap opera and the voice of fear. The Lord's voice never had a chance to be heard.

That's the difference in our lives when we spend time in His Word. We give it strength. We give it importance, and it changes how we respond to our situations.

It is important that we taste and experience who He says we are; we must believe and trust His Word over our feelings and over what the world may say, what Satan may be whispering in our ear, and what circumstances would lead us to believe.

"Jesus replied to them, 'I am the Bread of Life. The one who comes to Me will never be hungry, and the one who believes in Me [as Savior] will never be thirsty [for that one will be sustained spiritually]'" (John 6:35).

This is the Bride hearing the heartbeat of the Lord for her and living out of His truth for her, above and beyond what anything else would tell her. For the Bride to walk out in redemptive power, she must believe her Bridegroom above all other voices she may hear. She must seek her Bridegroom more diligently than anything else her soul may desire.

As the Bride, all you need to do is come. Be in your Bridegroom's presence. He is waiting. He longs to be with you, to laugh with you, to cry with you. He longs to be invited into your every moment.

Journal Entries

1/30/12

Good morning, Jesus. This is a beautiful day, a glorious day because of You. I have everything I need; everything that is required of me today is already mine. I praise You, Jesus. You are my beautiful Savior and everything I need! Praise You, Jesus. Blessing and honor and glory ascribe to Your Holy name. I love You, Lord, and I hunger for Your presence. I desire You and You alone. You are my breath, my life. I have life because of you, Jesus! I am alive because of You, Jesus!

Bride expects, and anticipates her Bridegroom will never let her down. In a difficult situation, He will be there to defend her, sustain her, rescue her. Not an engaged couple wondering how this is all going to work out, but He is my Bridegroom. The One I can depend on. He has never left me or forsaken me, and I can trust in His Word.

Psalm 34. Hallelujah, Jesus. I can trust You, lean on You. I require You, seek You, and You deliver me from all my fears (v4). My life makes its boasts in You; because of You, I have life. You:

deliver me from all my fears (v4);
make me glad (v2);
make me radiant and I will not be put to shame (v5) or
    be confused;
hear me and save me from all of my troubles (v6);
Angels encamp around me and deliver me (v7);
As I eat of Your Word, trust in You, I will know by
    experience You are good (v8);
I will have no want as I magnify Your name (v9);
I will lack nothing because I seek the Lord on the author-
    ity of His Word (v10).

When the righteous cry for help the Lord delivers them
out of distress and troubles (v17). The Lord is close to those
who are of a broken heart and saves those crushed from the
sorrow of sin because they are humble and penitent (18). The
Lord delivers us from evil (v19). The Lord is our Redeemer,
and no one who trusts in Him and takes refuge in Him shall
be condemned or held guilty (v22).
"I will bless the Lord at all times" (v1).
When my heart wants to complain, I will choose to bless
the Lord in all things, all the time. I receive His benefits, what
the Psalmist wrote as I turn my heart towards Him. I want
what the Psalmist wrote to be a reality in my life, "His praise
shall continually be in my mouth" (v1). Memorize Psalm 34:1,
"I will bless the Lord at all times; His praise shall continually
be in my mouth."

4/11/12

I saw myself with the Lord, and there was a ribbon, and each
of us held an end as if we were dancing around a Maypole. He
said, "I am always with you, and even if I send you out, we
are connected. It is a dance that you and I dance together. As
you fulfill your destiny, I am dancing with you because your

purpose is a dance with me; only you and I can perform it. I am yours, and you are mine. Hear the music and dance to the rhythm. Flow with the music. The steps have been ordained by Me, predestined by Me.

"I will never let you get out of step, out of My rhythm. As you spend time with Me, you will begin to hear the music more clearly, and the music will also flow from your heart; the rhythm will be a part of you. The music can't be heard by others because this is our dance set to our music. You will hear it, and you will be able to dance to it beautifully. As you look around, do not get confused if you are not dancing like others—they are dancing to other music or not hearing any music at all. Do not let your heart try to change the steps because it will be harder for you to hear the music of our hearts together. Keep your eyes on Me, your heart set on Me, and you will never be out of step."

"Your dance brings Me great joy. Healing flows, hearts are set free, provision is released. It's beautiful, and Heaven dances with you; angels dance with you. I love you, My darling child. Teach My children to dance with Me. Teach My children, My daughters, to hear the music of My heart for them. I have ribbons for every one of them. Some have picked them up only to lay them back down again. Others don't even know there is a ribbon for them, they long for it, but they don't know what it is or how to pick it up. Love them, My darling. Show them and teach them. I am with you."

Application Questions

1. To what or to whom do you turn for answers and truth?
2. What would it look like in your day if you turned to the Lord first for His Word for your manna?
3. In the first moments of difficulty, what do you turn to for truth and for a way out?

4. Think of a trying situation that you recently walked through. How would it have turned out differently if you had stood on God's truth for you in the midst of the situation?
5. Did you know God's truth for you in that situation?
6. What can you change so that you are trusting God's truth over the voice of your friend, the world, or the enemy? How do you discern between the voices?
7. Knowing now that Jesus longs to spend time with you, how will you satisfy both of your longings (Him for you and you for Him)?

SECTION 2

Preparing

After the Jewish marriage covenant had been established, the groom would leave the home of the bride and return to his father's house. There he would remain separate from his bride for twelve months. This period of separation afforded the bride time to gather her trousseau and to prepare for married life. The groom occupied himself by preparing the place that they would live within his father's house.

The *mikvah* is a ceremonial washing ritual the Bride performs during the time of preparation before her wedding. At the mikvah, a Bride fully immerses herself in water before the wedding. It may be the night before or as close to the wedding as possible. The mikvah brings the sense of rebirth and the new world that begins with marriage. The bride is connecting with the profound change marriage will bring to her life.

Ephesians 5:26–27 (AMPC) says, "So that He might sanctify her, having cleansed her by the washing of water with the Word, that He might present the church to Himself in glorious splendor, without spot or wrinkle or any such things [that she might be holy and faultless]."

As Christ's Bride, we are washed by Water, the Spirit, and the Word, Jesus. As we continue to trust the Lord, read His Word, and allow the Word to sanctify us and transform us, we are participating in the preparation. We can liken this time to the mikvah. This is when the Word cleanses us and sanctifies us; the Word brings about a profound transformation in our heart and our mind as we submit to it and allow it to do its work within us.

The washing of Christ's blood from the cross washes us clean from sin, guilt, condemnation, and shame. The washing of the Word is the time that we begin to believe the Word and receive it as complete and finished in our life here on this earth.

"You have been regenerated (born again), not from a mortal origin (seed, sperm), but from one that is immortal by the ever living and lasting Word of God" (1 Peter 1:23 AMPC).

"Who were chosen and foreknown by God the Father and consecrated (sanctified made holy) by the Spirit to be obedient to Jesus Christ (the Messiah) and to be sprinkled with [His] blood: May grace (spiritual blessing) and peace be given you in increasing abundance [that spiritual peace to be realized in and through Christ, freedom from fears, agitating passions, and moral conflicts]. Praised (honored, blessed) be the God and Father of our Lord Jesus Christ (the Messiah)! By His boundless mercy we have been born again to an ever-living hope through the resurrection of Jesus Christ from the dead" (1 Peter 1:2–3 AMPC).

During this process, we don't fully know what truths have taken root in our heart until difficulty comes. Those times reveal what is in our heart.

This is a good thing, though. God loves us so deeply in that time as we continue to draw near to Him; He will take the lies and unbelief out and replace it with truth. He already knows what is in our heart. When it comes out, it is for us to see and to deal with. If we don't know what we truly believe, then we are deceiving ourselves and are an easy landing strip for the enemy to touch down. God never condemns or puts us to shame. His grace and mercy abound and His Holy Spirit strengthens and purifies us so that we are continually transformed into His image and prepared to be His Bride. It is the transformed mind that faces every situation and knows that Jesus is more than enough. It is the transformed heart that believes Jesus is bigger than any problem or circumstance that comes our way.

The time of preparation is the privilege of learning how to stand in the authority of Christ against the tactics, schemes, and plans of the enemy. As His Bride, you are redeemed. You are everything He has called you to be in your "spirit man." Now is the time that your soul begins to catch up with the truth. You are a new creation. You are the Redeemed Bride of

Christ, no matter what you may have walked through. The Redemption of Christ is being worked out in you. It is a time to lay down your past identities and old way of doing things and discover your new identity in Him and how He says you are to walk through this life for Him and His Kingdom.

Through this time of preparation, you have the privilege of rising in strength, walking in authority, understanding what part of the world still clings to your heart and discover what you need to stand in truth. It's a process until we go to be with Him.

The enemy, Satan, attempts to take us out with persecution and trials. God is so much bigger than anything Satan can throw at us, and in His goodness, what Satan uses to attempt our destruction God uses to make us overcomers (Romans 8:28; 1 John 5:4; Romans 8:37)! God uses these things to make us stronger. He uses them so that we can believe in our heart what we know in our heads to be true. When we believe it in our heart, Satan is defeated in that area of our lives. The enemy has no access there.

This next section reveals keys to overcoming in our circumstances, as we continually submit ourselves to transformation. Everything we do in our walk with Christ is a process. Knowing what is available to us through Him and the power of His Spirit working in us is part of that process. Being content in our relationship with Christ, feeling comfortable with where we have our faith and how we live our life, keeps us from experiencing a deeper and more satisfying relationship with Him. Contentment in our faith and lack of knowledge don't protect us from being tossed around by the waves of circumstances that come out of nowhere and into our lives. Our stability and protection come from continuing to press in for more, becoming increasingly secured and anchored in the Word and His truth.

These keys will stir a desire in your heart to take hold of all that Christ has for you. May you become intentional during the time of preparation, so that in every area of your life you can be the overcoming redeemed Bride that the Bridegroom will be coming for.

CHAPTER 4

Words Create Our Experience

We have all experienced a storm. When it hits, our first reaction involves our emotions, our feelings. Our feelings come out of our soul, our experiences, our belief system. Emotions are very real, BUT that does not make them true. Our emotions can drag us around by our nose down a path of pain and hurt. They can make any circumstance into a roller coaster ride. Preparation for the storms in our lives has to be intentional, and it has to be done before times get hard.

Our first response will determine the road we travel as we walk through the circumstance. We have a choice at that moment. Knowing that our feelings may not tell us the truth can help us understand that we have a choice. One choice is to follow our emotions and the world's perspective when news and events come out of nowhere. This choice leads to pain and hurt. The other choice is to purposefully choose truth and be set free from the emotional roller coaster ride, and step onto the road to victory.

Our first words that we speak will open doors that lead us to peace, or lead us to fear and anxiety. The first door we choose will either make it easier or harder to hear the voice of truth. The longer we continue opening up doors to fear, the harder it will be to hear the voice that brings peace and truth to our situation.

Fear's voice becomes louder and louder.

The pictures that fear ingrains on our heart get clearer and clearer.

When we agree with the pictures we are seeing, they become the road we walk on.

This doesn't have to be the way we walk through difficult times or uncertain situations. We have the Word of God. When we use the Word of God and our experience of His love for us as our compass, we will not be moved, we will not be overcome. Instead, we will be the victors, and we will overcome in every situation. So, when fear whispers to our heart, we won't allow our thoughts to agree with it and become entangled.

We can silence fear by speaking God's truth over our circumstances.

As we speak His truth, our eyes are lifted up and hope and expectation flood our heart.

As hope floods our heart, we see how He has overcome for us, and how, with one step at a time, it will all be okay.

Peace floods our soul.

The pictures that expectation and peace paint upon our heart help us place one foot in front of the other, as we see Jesus meet us every step of the way.

We can seek His heart for our circumstances, and we can speak those words over our situation.

These words are our weapons. The Word of God is our weapon. It is a sword ready for battle.

To walk in victory, you must be prepared rather than scramble for the weapons or tools needed while you are in the midst of the battle. The beauty of sitting at Jesus' feet for preparation is that He knows exactly what you need before you need it. He knows the weapons you need in your arsenal.

When my husband first became sick, we thought it was just the flu, so we weren't that concerned. As the severity of the symptoms increased, he went to the internet for information. He discovered he needed to go to the emergency room immediately. The symptoms revealed that something more than the flu was going on inside him.

As he proceeded through the tests and procedures, little by little, we discovered what was hiding in his body. The doctors did not know the full extent until a procedure was performed to clear his bile duct. During this short hospital stay, we discovered what was going on inside of him.

I knew that my thoughts and my words were critical for me to remain in peace and in agreement with the Word of God. This is exactly what Ronnie and I did. It kept us in peace.

Isaiah 26:3 says, "You will keep in perfect and constant peace the one whose mind is steadfast [that is, committed and focused on You—in both inclination and character], because he trusts and takes refuge in You [with hope and confident expectation]."

When we went in for the follow-up doctor's appointment a few days after the procedure, I hadn't even planned on going. Ronnie looked and felt fine. He was running again in the morning and had no more symptoms. We had no idea that what we thought was over had only just begun.

I went to the appointment because he asked me to come. Just to be there with him to hear and understand the tests and procedures. Instead, what we heard was news that no one ever wants to hear. We saw it on the doctor's face when we first walked into the room. We could tell that this was not going to go as we expected. The soberness of his greeting to us and the desire to get right to the point revealed the seriousness of this meeting. The words we heard had the ability to rock us to our core and rip our insides out. The doctor very slowly and soberly told us, "The tests have come back on the cells that we removed. Ronnie has a very fast growing rare form of cancer. We recommend you go to Iowa City or Mayo immediately."

Thoughts began swirling in my head. My emotions took their seats and buckled themselves in for a roller coaster ride. My body began to react, my heart beating fast and my breathing becoming shallow.

Those words hit us like a brick. What was going on? Where did this come from?

If the Lord hadn't been preparing me each morning when I went to Him, I would have been a mess because of what those words had the power to do to my emotions. Though these words hit hard and my feelings responded, Jesus had shown me that these words were not truth.

My journal entry dated June 5, 2012, a month prior to the doctor's meeting, read:

John 19:30: "It is finished."

Luke 8:50, AMPC: "Do not be seized with alarm or struck with fear; simply believe [in Me as able to do this], and she will be made well."

Jairus, while in Jesus' presence, went to the One who was the source for his daughter's healing. Even there, he received bad news about his daughter that could have shaken his faith, but Jesus simply said to believe. Believe in Him who is able.

The enemy tries to get us off guard, shakes us even when we are going for the healing touch. May faith arise in God's people today to simply believe and not be moved by whatever the enemy's report to us is—it is <u>not</u> God's report about our situation! God says it is finished (John 19:30).

The Lord was showing me in His Word on that day how He wanted me to stand in Him. Little did I know at that time that in only a few short weeks I would need to choose the truth I would believe about my husband's health.

Would I believe Jesus' Words from Luke that He was able to take care of us, or would I believe the doctor's words?

Would I believe and speak out loud the whispers of fear that erupted and wanted to take over my thoughts from the medical diagnosis? Would I agree with my spiraling emotions whirling around inside of me?

Just because I was feeling a whirlwind of emotion didn't mean I would allow them freedom and access to become my thoughts. Agreement meant access, and I needed to make a choice about what I was going to agree with.

As we heard the doctor's diagnosis, we had to breathe. We grabbed each other's hand and spoke the words for where we needed to stand. The thoughts hounding us would not have the opportunity to make paths for us to travel down if we did not speak them. So instead, we spoke what we knew of the Lord.

"God's got this."

"This is not the final word. God has the final Word."

"He is bigger than any statistic that man can calculate."

"We will choose to keep our eyes on Him and not be moved by these words."

Being there in unity helped us both to be strong.

Agreeing with the Lord didn't mean that we did nothing in the natural world. Agreeing with the Lord meant that we would create with our thoughts and words the road we were going to traverse in this journey.

Before we left the doctor's office, we made an appointment at Mayo Clinic for a few weeks later. The journey was beginning.

As we drove home separately from the appointment, my heart turned to the Lord. I knew that keeping my thoughts in agreement with the Lord was not a one-time shot. Instead, I knew that my thoughts and feelings would continue to swirl, and it would be an ongoing process not to agree with them.

I knew I had to rein in my thoughts from going down the road the doctor's words had prepared for us to travel. Hopelessness was knocking and trying to come in. The key to getting control was to choose immediately the road I wanted and just keep bringing my thoughts back around again each time they began to wander.

I had been learning to control my thoughts on the smaller things in life. This was a big one, though. My thoughts had no desire to be controlled, so I felt uncomfortable reining them in. It would have been much easier just to let them go. The pictures that those feelings wanted for my future were easy to paint. They were gathering information from what the doctor said and from what I had heard happened to other people in our same situation. So much of this world was giving my emotions and thoughts information to paint those hopeless pictures.

We want to know what is going to happen. The unknown is very hard for us. When our thoughts, fears, and emotions paint the future for us, it is very uncomfortable to say "no" to them because they are making an unknown future known, even if it isn't a good future.

If our feelings and emotions don't like to be reined in or aren't used to being reined in, they will not go quietly. As you choose to speak and believe God's Words, you are breaking new ground, and it can even feel like you are plowing a hard, dry field.

Stopping the thoughts and emotions from taking over required an experience of the Lord's love for me. If I had not experienced the depth of His love for me several years earlier, I would not have been able to look at fear and tell it to go. I would not have been confident enough in His love for me to stand firm. I may have begun questioning if He even loved me.

1 John 4:18 says, "There is no fear in love [dread does not exist], but full-grown (complete, perfect) love turns fear out of doors and expels every trace of terror! For fear brings with it the thought of punishment, and [so] he who is afraid has not reached the full maturity of love [is not yet grown into love's complete perfection]."

In this time of preparation, situations come at us that reveal the depth of love we operate in. It's not the depth of my love, it is the depth of my agreement and faith in His love for me. The more we are confident in His love and the more we receive it in our situation, fear will have to flee.

So I put my eyes on Jesus and magnified the Lord and not my problem. I wanted to stay with the Lord's truth and hope right from the start. I needed to hear His heart for us in this situation. I needed to know what He had to say about Ronnie's diagnosis. I spoke to Him about how good He is, and told Him I needed Him here, right now, to speak truth to my heart.

> It's not the depth of my love, it is the depth of my agreement and faith in His love for me.

As I looked to the Lord, a song rose within me, a song from my childhood that I hadn't sung in years, "On Christ the Solid Rock I Stand All Other Ground is Sinking Sand."

I began singing the verses as best I could, and my faith was stirred up. I knew that I was standing on solid ground.

I could now call my best friend and prayer warrior, Kate. Jesus and I stood together—He had given me what I needed, and now I wanted to let her know what we had heard and where we were standing so that she could stand with us in prayer. Kate could not have given me the peace that Jesus had given to me. Of course, her words would have brought encouragement, but it is only the Word of Jesus that can give a sure foundation against whatever may come crashing against you.

Amazingly, one of the first things she asked me was if I knew the song, "On Christ the Solid Rock I Stand"? I almost had to pull over on the side of the road. Incredible. Jesus was so good that He confirmed what He had told me through her. This is who my Jesus is. This is how He wanted me to stand, knowing that He was our rock, and everything else would swallow us up in sinking sand. The doctor's diagnosis, the fear, the statistics—nothing would give us the solid rock to stand firm and unwavering, except Jesus.

We had the opportunity to talk about what the doctor said, repeat the hopelessness of the diagnosis, become scared, and call everyone we knew and repeat with our words everything that we heard. When we do this, we are creating the path in front of us that we will have to walk. You might say, "But you are ignoring reality." No, our words agree with the truth we know from God's Word. What good is it to know intellectually that God heals and He is our anchor and hope, if when news comes we completely forget His truth and fill our thoughts and words with what the bad news is saying?

There is friction, opposing forces that will come against what the Word of God says. We cannot expect that our earthly experience will come alongside us and agree with what we are learning at Jesus' feet. As I learn more of the truths from the Word, my experiences in this world attempt to steal that understanding from me. My experiences are giving me an opportunity to take my understanding and make it my actions. As we stand on the Word of God instead of the reality of this world, it changes from an intellectual understanding into a heart knowing.

This is not denial; this is the beginning of grabbing hold of the truth and making it our own, taking the truth and turning it into an experience of Jesus. This is the love of the Bride. This is how the Bride begins to become one with her Bridegroom; she becomes one with the Word who is her Bridegroom. She aligns her thoughts, aligns her words with His Word, and as she speaks His truth into her situation she continues to stay aligned with Him. Her emotions that want to go on a wild roller coaster ride are brought into submission by her words and aren't even given a chance to cause her to be tossed to and fro.

As we waited for our appointment at Mayo Clinic, Ronnie and I kept our eyes firmly on Jesus. We confronted the words from the doctor's visit with the truth of Jesus. We had great expectation and hope for the Lord's healing in Ronnie's body. We were standing on the solid ground we had found in Jesus.

Journal Entries

7/6/12

"On Christ the solid rock I stand; all other ground is sinking sand!" Kate and I both got this song as report was given yesterday. Praise God, He is our solid rock. He is Ronnie's solid rock. As the Lord finishes the work of unblocking in natural and spiritual ways, I praise God we pressed in for more. I thank You, Lord. Ronnie receives his *rhema* and *logos* Word directly from our Father's heart by Your Spirit. Hallelujah, breakthrough is coming!

Psalm 103; Psalm 15. Walking in Lord's righteousness, living for Him, we shall not be moved.

Psalm 16. He instructs us in the night season and in His presence is fullness of joy and at His right hand are pleasures for evermore.

Hebrews 2:8–9. The Father created us and put everything in subjection to man. We don't see that yet, the manifestation of it, but we do see Jesus. And everything has been put under the feet of Jesus and it is through Him that we can see what has not yet been made manifest!

7/16/12

Last night driving and talking to the Lord about how hard it is and how this world is tough and ugly, I felt Him say, "You need to bring the truth of Jesus of Heaven into all those circumstances. I can't do it without you." I realized that I agree with the enemy in everyday situations far more often than I do with Jesus. Every time I feel frustration, hurt, anger, jealousy that begins to rise, I have a choice to agree with it or say no and reach into my spirit to rise up and bring forth truth, Your truth.

As frustration and anger have "risen" from my soul, may the power of Jesus rise up in me from my spirit. One is from my soul that I have felt all my life; I am a new creation, and may Jesus rise up from my spirit, same rising up, and may it be powerful for the Kingdom. Out of my belly will flow rivers of living water. Water that refreshes and brings forth truth and releases life, words, thoughts that are life, life to me and life to others around me, and life to every situation and circumstance! Praise You, Jesus! I worship You, Lord. My day lies before me and I have choices of life and death. I choose life today, Lord, for far too long I have chosen death, even in small areas of my life. I choose Your truth this day, Lord, Your truth Your way, Your Words. May Your Spirit flow in and through me this day.

Application Questions

1. Remembering a difficult situation, what were the first words that came out of your mouth? Looking back on it now, what doors did those words open up for you to walk through?
2. What words of life could you have spoken instead? Can you "see" the doors that would have been closed by these words? Can you "see" the doors that would have been opened by these words?
3. What can you do to prepare yourself now for speaking words of life when the storm first hits?
4. In what area of your life can you apply the truth of the Word to begin seeing victory?

CHAPTER 5

Remaining in Hope

Hope. Without hope, we cannot see that things can change tomorrow. Hopelessness blinds us to see only our current circumstances. Hopelessness, just like fear, takes us down a road of thinking things will never get better—they will just continue to get worse or will never change. Without hope, we are unable to see that how we respond to the situation has an effect on how we walk through the situation.

Hope that is anchored in the situation isn't hope at all.

True hope is a person, and His name is Jesus Christ.

When we trust in Jesus, who is our anchor of hope, our hope is not based upon what is happening in our situation. Our hope is rooted in who He is and all that He has done for us.

As we hope in Jesus, things may not change in an instant, but we are guaranteed that they will change. Our situation can't help but change. Our biggest breakthrough is usually right on the other side of what seems like our most hopeless moment.

"[What, what would have become of me] had I not believed that I would see the Lord's goodness in the land of the living! Wait and hope for and expect the Lord; be brave and of good courage and let your heart be stout and enduring. Yes, wait for and hope for and expect the Lord" (Psalm 27:13–14 AMPC).

An expectation of the Lord in the midst of our circumstances gives room for Him to come in. Expectation helps us to see what He is doing because we are watching for Him to come.

Hope keeps dread away and sees the impossible as possible. Disbelief comes when we choose to see only the brokenness of the moment and not the hope of a new future. Hope is the positive use of your imagination. We all have an imagination and see pictures as we think and speak with others. Hope uses our imagination and then faith brings it forth. If hope hasn't perceived it, faith can't receive it.

"Do not [earnestly] remember the former things; neither consider the things of old. Behold, I am doing a new thing! Now it springs forth; do you not perceive and know it, and will you not give heed to it? I will even make a way in the wilderness and rivers in the desert" (Isaiah 43:18–19 AMPC).

As we put our trust in Him and Him alone, He becomes our dependency. Then our dependency becomes our ascendency.

"But those who wait for the Lord [who expect, look for, and hope in Him] shall change and renew their strength and power; they shall lift their wings and mount up [close to God] as eagles [mount up to the sun]; they shall run and not be weary, they shall walk and not faint or become tired" (Isaiah 40:31 AMPC).

Hoping and waiting can feel like a very long, drawn-out circumstance. In the past, when I have thought about waiting, I think of a desert where I see nothing but sand all around me, and I'm just trudging on with no joy, the days passing one after another with nothing changing. Religion would say that this is a place that I will learn about my Savior. Religion says that this can be a good place to walk through because everyone must walk through these times in order to grow in faith and patience.

Hope says otherwise. Hope says that as we wait upon the Lord, we will rise in strength. Hope says that this is a time of basking in the beauty of who Christ is and all that He has done for us. Hope says that we can expect our situation to change at any moment.

Psalm 119:81 says, "My soul languishes and grows weak for Your salvation; I wait for your Word."

My soul, will, emotions, and thinking grow faint waiting for Jesus and all that He has for me. I put my hope in His Word. My hope is not in what I'm waiting for. My hope is in Jesus and his truth.

Psalm 119:89 says, "Forever, O Lord, Your word is settled in Heaven [standing firm and unchangeable]."

God's Word is already settled in Heaven. It is unchangeable and stands firm so we can wait on Him, and we can trust Him to be faithful in what He has said.

As our strength rises while we wait, we also know that the joy of the Lord is our strength (Nehemiah 8:10). So as strength rises, joy bubbles up from within us. The only source that says waiting is a dry place is this world, because waiting with no hope is a dry place. We are Christ's own, and we have Him as our anchor of hope, so waiting on Him is a place of great strength and joy, filled with expectation.

You may say, "But I don't feel any strength or joy as I wait. I don't even have any hope." These are your feelings, and they are not truth. We must train our soul (mind, will, and emotions) to what is truth. Every time that you get dragged down and hopelessness takes over, speak the Word of God over yourself. Declare what Jesus says about your situation. Jesus never intended for us to take our emotions, that keep us out of His peace, to the other side of the cross.

> Jesus never intended for us to take our emotions, that keep us out of His peace, to the other side of the cross.

49

During this time of preparation, remember, the Bride is preparing herself. We cannot step into the new relationship with our old emotions and old way of thinking and doing. If the old way was good enough, we would not have to spend time preparing. This is a time that we rid ourselves of things of this world and live out of the truth of the Word. Rather than our emotions telling us how to respond in a given situation, we seek the Word and come into agreement with the way the Word says we live, breathe, and respond to our situations and the world around us.

"Return to the stronghold [of security and prosperity], you prisoners of hope, even today do I declare that I will restore double your former prosperity to you" (Zechariah 9:12 AMPC).

Where are we to reside? In the stronghold of security and prosperity, which can only be found in the Lord. He is our strong tower, He is our refuge, and we are held under His wings. He is the Word. The Word is where we find strength and shelter from the storms of this world. His Word is where we find truth that tells us how we are to move and breathe and believe (Psalm 61:3; Proverbs 18:10; Psalm 91:4).

Jesus knows our every emotion. He has compassion and feels our pain. He took our sorrows on the cross so that we might have gladness and joy (Isaiah 53; 35:10; 51:11; Matthew 8:17). This is our truth, and during this time of preparation, we encourage ourselves and each other to give Jesus our feelings and our hopelessness so that we might live in the hope and joy that He has for us—no matter the situation. Hope is a ladder that has steps of faith, strength, and joy.

The few weeks leading up to our appointment at Mayo Clinic passed by quickly. We soon found ourselves on the road to what we believed would be the answer to what was hidden inside Ronnie. We were expecting to have consultations with the doctors, and then a more in-depth cleaning of Ronnie's bile duct so the cells could be quickly eradicated.

After Ronnie's doctor's consultation at home, he began to look back at how he had felt over the prior 12 months. In retrospect, he could see symptoms that were red flags now but at that time didn't seem to mean that much. He had documented the entire 12 months and the symptoms and was convinced that sharing these with the doctors at Mayo would help them understand that this was not as severe as they were telling us.

If you have gone through a journey of illness, you may have experienced what happened to us the very first day at our first appointment. Things were not as we'd expected.

We thought Ronnie would undergo a quick procedure and then we'd be on our way home. The fact that we were at Mayo was wonderful, because not only would Ronnie get this behind him, but we would be able to pray for others and bring hope in difficult situations. We did have opportunities to pray for others even before we arrived at the Clinic. Most of the hotels around Mayo are used by the patients and their families. On our way to the clinic that first morning we rode down the elevator with a family heading to their appointment. We were able to talk to them about the Lord's healing power and pray over the mother before we got into our respective cars. Being able to minister to others helped us take the focus off of ourselves.

At our first appointment, we didn't have to wait long to be called back by one of the assistants. She immediately asked us to consider having Ronnie be a part of the research for his cancer. She handed us the forms and left the room. Ronnie and I looked at each other, shocked, and all we could say was, "No." We discussed how everything this assistant said to us was contrary to what our doctors had told us at home. We decided that she must not understand Ronnie's case, and we would get this all cleared up when we saw the doctor.

When the doctor came in, the conversation was more in the line of us getting on the same page as Mayo. Contrary to what our doctors had told us, Mayo Clinic's only treatment was a reconstruction surgery that was high risk but had great outcomes.

Appointment after appointment, Ronnie would share his health journey with the doctor, and they would explain that none of that really mattered at this point. Ronnie was an electrical engineer, brilliant and very logical. That is why he was so successful in his career. His analytical background, though highly useful when he created new technologies at work, was only causing a stumbling block between ourselves and the doctors. It took several appointments before we caught up to where they were, and Ronnie finally laid down his 12 months of medical information.

Staying hopeful during these few days was a constant battle of our thoughts. We had no expectation of receiving the news we were given, and so we had to continually encourage each other and talk about what God was doing in the midst of all these conversations and procedures.

Our last appointment of those few days was a gift from the Lord. The doctor we were assigned for the surgery was one of the few in the world that performed the surgery laparoscopically. He went over all the tests with us and said that Ronnie was in excellent health and so much better than the rest of his patients. By the time this cancer is usually discovered, most patients are already very sick so that the surgery and recovery become more difficult and challenging. He told us that Ronnie would have a quick surgery and would live a long and healthy life.

We left that day feeling so uplifted on our drive home. We talked about how good God was to give Ronnie the very best surgeon, and that he spoke only words of life over him. Even though we were not expecting to receive the news we did, it ended with hope and expectation of God's goodness for Ronnie. Even though they would be removing his bile duct and doing reconstruction surgery to attach his small intestine to his gall bladder to function as the bile duct, we knew that having this surgeon was a gift from the Lord. Not needing anything more than a few cuts would be so much better than a surgery where his abdomen would be cut open with one large incision.

We had scheduled the surgery a few weeks out so that we could finish up our son Daniel's traveling basketball tournaments and celebrate Ronnie's birthday. We were filled with the expectation of having all of this behind us soon, with the exception of the 6-week recovery time. Ronnie set everything up with work so that he could work from home and not travel over those 6 weeks. We arranged for Daniel to stay with friends, but our daughter Lydia came with us. She was only 9 and didn't do well being apart from us during the first trip to Mayo. We also thought she would be a great distraction, and it would help to have her with us during this trip.

Hope and expectation of all that God was doing even in the midst of cancer and surgery carried us through and gave us strength to move forward.

My journal entry on July 26, 2012, four days before surgery:
Praise lifts me high above the troubles, helps me to hear and love others, accepting and covering wrongs. Praise keeps me in His presence, and the troubles aren't troubles because He is far better than being dragged down by them or into the midst of them. My needs are completely satisfied as I praise Him. It's like I come into a safe enclosed environment and

every need within me is satisfied, every dry place quenched by His spirit, every fleshly desire burned up by His Spirit. It's not a place of "I'll ignore you," but a place of abiding with my eyes beholding the beauty of Jesus, the position of Jesus, my Father's heart towards me and the power of that truth invading and overtaking what I see with my natural eyes and what I experience. I have a choice today. I can stay in His presence, magnifying His Holy name and being completely satisfied by Him. Or I can be sucked out of that place by agreeing with the enemy that what I see, hear, taste, smell, touch is greater than the truth of Jesus in every situation, conversation, circumstance.

The day of the surgery we were to arrive early at the hospital so Ronnie could be prepped. He wasn't the first patient on the doctor's surgery list that day, and the earlier surgery took longer than expected, so we had to wait a few hours before they could wheel Ronnie back to the operating room. As we waited, the television hanging in the corner of the room was a mere distraction from our conversation that would ebb and flow. We talked about the kids and how great it would be for this to be behind us. We marveled at how good God was to bring this great surgeon into our lives and all the other wonderful things that God was doing, big and small.

We did relatively well keeping our thoughts off anything that would bring fear. Not putting words to what was on our minds helped negative thoughts to keep on running right out the door without us. Ronnie wasn't too nervous, but the longer we waited, the harder it was to ignore what we were waiting for.

Finally, it was Ronnie's turn to be wheeled back. The doctor was finishing up the previous surgery. The operating nurses came to wheel Ronnie to another waiting room where Lydia and I were not allowed to enter. Instead, the floor nurses took us to his post-op room. As we were getting situated, we were told it could be a while before Ronnie's surgery would even start. They encouraged us to get a bite to eat before we settled in for the 5–6-hour surgery.

Lydia and I went to lunch outside the hospital, and when we returned the surgery assistant came to the room. She said that the doctor wanted to meet with me. I asked her how long Ronnie had actually been undergoing surgery. She said that he had been in about 45 minutes. I was shocked but full of hope that it was great news. Lydia and I followed the assistant to the surgery consultation room.

We began the walk down the long, sterile hallway. Even though a few moments ago I was thinking of only the best news, suddenly every possible scenario bombarded me. It was as if I was pushing my way down a hallway crowded with horrible thoughts, but once I got past one, there were dozens more waiting to grab hold of my mind and take me down roads of hopelessness and fear.

The white walls helped illuminate the path. There was no one else around, just the surgery assistant, Lydia, and myself. The only sound was our shoes as we made our way down the hallway.

I began talking with the Lord in my heart because a conversation between the three of us seemed out of place. There was nothing in the hallway to grab my attention, and my heart needed to hold on to something even though I was holding onto my daughter's hand. So, I put my thoughts on the Lord and asked for His healing power in my husband's body.

I asked the Lord, "Why are we able to talk to the doctor so soon?"

I heard a whisper in my heart, "It's all going to be okay."

That was all I needed to hear. Peace flooded my soul like a warm liquid flowing down over me. What felt like chaos in my thoughts was suddenly wrapped up in trusting stillness. I repeated what I had heard, "Yes Jesus, it is all going to be okay. Thank You for being here with us, thank You for the answer to our prayers for the quick and easy surgery for Ronnie. Thank you for never leaving us or forsaking us. It's all going to be okay."

This hallway to the surgery consultation room was the transition for me from the place of learning at Jesus' feet to where I had to begin living it out. I was unaware at that moment that the turbulent winds were blowing, attempting to grab hold of me and carry me away. I had no idea that the understanding I had of Jesus as the anchor of my hope would soon be the only anchor I had to hold on to.

We were told to sit in a little room and wait for the doctor. The space was more like a cubicle with a door than a room. My heart kept beating faster and faster the longer we waited, the walls beginning to close in on me. Suddenly the door opened, and the doctor walked in. He looked at me very seriously and then saw my little Lydia. His countenance changed; it seemed like seeing Lydia made him sad. Maybe I was misreading him because of all the emotions that were swirling around the room and bombarding my heart.

The doctor slowly told us that he had begun the laparoscopic procedure and was very surprised at what he saw. Inside of Ronnie were webs and sheets of cancer cells that wrapped around his bile duct, his pancreas, a main artery and into his liver.

He was so sorry, so very sorry. He had not expected this at all; there were no signs of the cancer being this advanced. He did not open him up because he knew that he could not cut any of the cancer away. If he did, he would only be cutting the cancerous cells open and allowing them to ravage even more of his body. His surgery assistants were in the process of stitching up the small incisions in his abdomen. He was so sorry there was nothing that he could do. He continually looked at Lydia, and I could tell he was choosing his words very carefully so as not to upset her.

Though he tried not to say too much, what he had just said was more than my heart could handle. I needed to get to a quiet place to digest the thoughts that were swirling and screaming inside my heart and head. I didn't cry or get upset because I couldn't even process what he was telling me. I thanked him and told him how we appreciated all that he had wanted to do for Ronnie. He asked me if I wanted to tell Ronnie or if I wanted him to break the news. I said that I wanted him to come to Ronnie's room after he awoke from anesthesia and talk to him about it. He said he would be there as soon as he could.

He got up and left the tiny room, leaving me alone with all of my thoughts and emotions running around those four little walls. Swirling, swirling. I couldn't take it all in, especially with my little Lydia looking at me and asking me how her daddy was.

The surgery assistant who had brought us here came back. When the door opened, it felt like the pressure that was mounting and swirling in the room was released all at once with a whoosh. She looked at us with sadness and said that she would take us back to Ronnie's room.

When we arrived at Ronnie's room, the nurse came to tell us that they had moved him to a private room so we could have privacy when he returned. The nurses were all so kind, but also looking at us with sad eyes, speaking to us in gentle voices. I knew then that they all knew what had happened, and they were feeling sorry for us. It was a terrible emotion to add to everything that was weighing on my heart. Now people were feeling sorry for us.

I settled Lydia in a chair with the television so that I could go to an empty waiting room and process with the Lord. I needed the Lord right then more than I ever did. I wanted to scream. I wanted to yell, "NO." I wanted to wake up. I kept thinking, *"This can't be.* We didn't come here for this news." Ronnie was going to be okay. He couldn't have all this cancer inside him. He had been running and feeling fine. The scans never showed anything in his body. A web of cancer covering all of his insides—how could this be?

"How could this have been hidden, Lord? You must be doing a great work of healing in his body, and it just hasn't manifested yet."

I had phone calls to make. I called our son, Ben, Ronnie's sister, Barb, my friend, Kate, and my parents. Talk about hard phone calls. I informed them of what the doctor had told me and then I told them that my God had the last word about Ronnie. I cried, but then I stood up in hope and expectation. I knew who my God was. Praying with Kate helped stir me up in faith. I would need it because Ronnie would be coming back soon and he would have no idea what had happened in surgery. How do I sit with my husband while knowing the truth, yet having to wait to tell him?

I went back to Ronnie's room to be with Lydia. I began to hear commotion and conversation in the hallway. They were wheeling Ronnie's bed into the room. My mind was racing with how I had to maintain peace, speak encouraging words, and somehow not tell Ronnie anything about the surgery.

I'll never forget his face when he saw me. He wasn't wearing his glasses, and he was just coming out of anesthesia, so his eyes were open wide, trying to focus. He was struggling to see and, trying to understand what was happening at the same time. He asked how long he was in surgery. I told him he had only been gone a few hours, in an attempt to avoid discussing any specifics. The nurses were adjusting tubes, bedding, and talking with him about what he could and could not do. It was good to have the noise of their conversation and not the silence of our room.

As the nurses left, I sat with Ronnie and held his hand, talking to him about how he was feeling and what Lydia and I had been doing while he was gone. It was interesting that he never asked me about the surgery. It was as if he knew something wasn't right and he just couldn't get himself to ask.

I told Ronnie that the surgeon would be coming to talk to us about the surgery very soon. We waited, sometimes in silence and sometimes with only small talk between us. It was getting very hard for me to keep the truth from him. It didn't seem right—like I was lying to him. We had never kept anything from each other. In our marriage, we were able to share openly about everything.

I went out several times to the nurses' station to find out when the surgeon would be coming. Over an hour had passed since Ronnie was wheeled into the room, and it was getting more difficult to remain silent by the moment. I kept talking in my heart to the Lord.

"How am I supposed to sit here, Lord? Will I have to tell Ronnie? Oh Lord, how could this possibly be? I must have fallen asleep. Wake me up from this nightmare, Lord."

Not knowing what to do with myself, my hands fell back in my lap, and my fingers touched the leather bracelet my friend Jane had given me before we left for the surgery. I looked down at the verse that was attached, "Simply Believe." When Jane had given it to me, she had no idea that this was from the Scripture that the Lord had shown me back in June, several weeks before we knew that Ronnie was sick. It was confirmation to me again that my role now was to simply believe in the One who was able.

Now I was able to look at Ronnie and encourage him with words of truth from the Lord. We talked about how good

God was and how He was our healer, Ronnie's healer. Peace flooded the room that chaos and fear had tried to control. God's truth never changes—it only changes me, my vision, and my thoughts.

With peace filling us, we finally talked about the elephant in the room. Ronnie was the first to speak. He wanted to know how everything had gone and why it was such a short surgery.

I started to cry and tell him I was so sorry. I wanted the surgeon to talk to him. I explained why the surgery was so short and what I understood they had found when they opened him up. I also remember telling him again that it didn't matter what they may have found or what they might say, God has the final Word, and He is our Healer.

All he could do was stare back at me. I'm not sure how much he understood because his mind was still groggy from the anesthesia.

The nurse came in and said the doctor was on his way. Ronnie and I looked at each other. I squeezed his hand and smiled.

In my heart, I prayed, "Lord, don't let him speak any words over Ronnie that are not in agreement with Your truth."

When the doctor arrived, he looked so sad. He glanced around the room, saw Lydia, and then took a deep breath and began to share. As he drew pictures on the whiteboard of what he found inside, he never spoke a death sentence over Ronnie but continued to say he was sorry and that he hadn't thought he would find cancer at this stage. He said, once again, that he couldn't cut any of it out because that would have only released the cells into his abdominal cavity and spread the cancer that much faster.

He said that Ronnie could either go back to the hotel and stay with us or remain in the hospital for the night. He would set up an appointment with an oncologist to discuss our options.

I praised God that he never spoke a timeline over Ronnie's life. It was a blessing for us in the days ahead that we never had to fight those words as Ronnie believed the Lord for his healing.

The doctor left, and Ronnie and I decided that it would be better for him to stay the night in the hospital so he could receive pain meds if he needed them. Lydia and I returned to the hotel room to get some rest.

In the morning, I arose and went to the Word. My bracelet with the words "Simply Believe" was still on my wrist, and I wanted to go back to the Scriptures that the Lord had given me to prepare me for the days ahead. I read again the story of Jesus in the eighth chapter of Luke with Jairus asking Him to heal his daughter. It was amazing to me that Jairus could stand in Jesus' presence, yet bad news was still able to come to him. That morning I knew the power that bad news can have on us. As I looked at the verse again, I was strengthened by the words of Jesus, as He too had heard what the servant had come to tell Jairus. We may not have had a servant come to us, but we had doctors say there was nothing they could do. Jesus' response to Jairus was, "Simply believe." I knew that Jesus' response to us was the same. "Simply believe."

Hope and faith stirred in me that morning. As I spoke with friends who wanted to check in and pray with me, I told them what the Lord was telling me. I continued to be stirred up with hope as I shared the Words from Jesus. Those words were what I stood on that day as I packed up our belongings and headed back to the hospital to get Ronnie and go to our appointment.

How do we remain in hope when the storm increases in volume and strength? We keep our eyes on Jesus. As Ronnie and I continued to hear the words from the doctors, we knew who had the last word. We remained on the firm foundation of hope and truth as the wind whipped around us. Being able to stand in hope comes from the preparation of knowing that God is good. We invite His truth into the very midst of our experience. Remaining in hope is a choice, choosing to disagree with the emotions or the words that come from a worldly view. One moment at a time, one thought at a time, we capture them and take them captive to Christ and His truth.

We are to live our life according to our faith. Circumstantial pressure comes from Satan. As we continue to respond to our life out of faith and truth, we will not be moved by Satan's lies. In Hebrews 11:3, we learn that God framed the world with words. We are to frame our world with our words to make a pathway for our tomorrow. The words that the doctors speak can release fear, and fear begins to imagine and rob us of hope. It is so important to grab hold of those words and take them captive to the truth of Christ.

What are the words that you are repeating as you walk through the storm? Are you repeating the words that stir up the storm? Agree with the storm? Or are you hearing those words and choosing to take your thoughts and eyes off them and put your eyes on Jesus?

The doctor's words had the potential and opportunity to take away every last drop of hope that we had, but only if we were hoping in man and his ability. When we walk through the storms as the Bride, we must be so passionately in love that we laugh at the words of others and wait for the Words of our Lover. His Words are the only ones that bring hope. His Words are the only ones that bring life. His Words are the only ones that make peace in the chaos. He is our hope. He is our rock.

Journal Entry 8/1/12

Lord, I don't know what my tomorrow will be, but I know it's going to be great in You. I am excited and expectant for our miracles and the transformations You have in store for us. The enemy has overplayed his hand, and we will be and are victorious over him. Jesus, it's because of You, Jesus. I worship You and bless Your Holy name.

The Lord spoke to me at service tonight and told me never to doubt that He will heal Ronnie, and He is putting a guard over my heart, a shield to protect me. Earlier in the day, the Lord said that "He is the one holding up my arms" because He is my strength.

In worship, the Lord told Ronnie that "He is putting a tent over our bed, bedroom," and may it be the tent of His presence where Ronnie's spirit will commune with the very presence of the Lord.

Our follow-up appointment with the doctor at Mayo before leaving connected us to an oncologist back home. There was nothing more that Mayo could do for Ronnie; they told us that his only hope for living a little longer would be to balance strong chemotherapy with his quality of life.

Many of us have faced a situation in this world where there is no hope, and there are no answers. I want you to know that because of He who lives in you there is always hope. We can live our days in the midst of bad news with hope and expectation because of who Christ is for us.

James Goll, the author of *Finding Hope*[1], states,

"Hope will secure our emotions, which crash like wild waves inside our souls and threaten to drown us. Hope is the strong and trustworthy anchor for our souls. In an unstable, impermanent, ever-changing world, hope fastens us to the bedrock of God, the Rock of Ages. Within the sanctuary of God, anchored firmly on him, we are safer than ever—safer, believe it or not, than before the storm engulfed us."

It is not the outcome that we are hoping for, believing for, praying for, holding onto—it is Jesus Christ the solid rock, the anchor of our soul. He never changes; He is faithful and true. Those who trust in Him will never be put to shame.

As we lean on Him and hope in Him come what may, it will be okay. Everything is going to be all right. The end of the story is that you overcome, you win. As we walk through trials, we don't put our hope on the results but in Christ.

I have a friend who is walking through storms in her life. As she talks to me about her struggles to trust Jesus for healing, she says she is scared to believe because if healing doesn't come on this side of Heaven, she will struggle with her faith in Jesus more than if she didn't believe for it.

This is founded on fear and hopelessness. This is not trusting that Jesus is more than enough. And as she walks through this storm, she will miss out on all that the Lord has for her and her family. Jesus has peace, mercy, grace, hope, and expectation. He is worth trusting. It is not the outcome we are trusting, but rather the One who holds our lives in His hands. We are trusting and hoping in the One who has already provided everything we need to get through to the other side.

Ronnie and I were told there was nothing more anyone could do. The cancer had gone too far. Instead of holding onto these words and allowing them to repeat over and over again in our heads, we went to the Lord and asked Him for His final Word. We lifted our eyes and looked to Him.

Every time that the doctor's words would come into my head, I would say,

"No, this is not Your final Word, Lord."

"You have said that by the stripes of Jesus, Ronnie was healed." (Isaiah 53:5)

"You said that those who hoped in You would never be put to shame."

"You said that You would never leave us or forsake us."

"You said that Your plans for us are good. We choose to look to You for those good plans even in the midst of what doctors are saying to us. We look to You."

To remain in hope, we didn't tell everyone about what the doctors were saying. We confided only in the people who would not look to those words but to the Lord along with us and press in for His healing for Ronnie.

Hope is the expectation of something good happening to you today. As the Bride of Christ, knowing of our Bridegroom's love for us, we can get up each day and be expectant, be hopeful. My favorite book says that each day is a brand new day filled full of grace and mercy just for that day. As we live in expectant hope, we are in a place to receive all Jesus has for us. With our eyes looking up, we are always ready and fully aware of what the Lord is doing. We are not looking to our situation, not rolling around in hopelessness but looking to Him.

Several years ago, as a leader in our Bible study, I had the opportunity to share about the woman in the Bible who had been hunched over for eighteen years (Luke 10:10–13). The leaders were taking turns speaking about the different women in the study. I was not thrilled the week that I had to talk about this woman because there were only a few verses about her. I wondered what I was going to talk about for 30 minutes. My friend Kate suggested that I take one day and live this woman's life. So I did.

I learned a lot about how my perspective on my life is affected by where I put my eyes. As I had my eyes constantly on my feet and the floor, I couldn't see where I was going. I had my eyes continually on the floor and the dirt. When I had a conversation with someone, I couldn't even look into their eyes. Not looking at someone can bring me into unworthiness and negative thoughts. I couldn't even look up to see the beautiful sunny day. I knew it was sunny, but instead of seeing the beauty it created I could only see the dirt it was highlighting on my floor.

Day after day, this woman lived like this. One day was enough for me. I can't imagine what it was like for her to live like that for 18 years. When Jesus called out to her in the crowd, she didn't even have the ability to look into His face and see love shining in His eyes.

By continually looking at our problem or circumstance and not up and outside of it to the heart and face of Jesus, we will stay in the captivity of the situation. Our perspective will not be filled with hope because we can't see hope. We can't see anything but the problem. We have the choice to look into the face of our Savior. We are His, and no matter where we might be or what others might have said, we can look deeply into His eyes and experience His love for us.

It is so important to know His heart for you, so that even in hopeless situations you will believe that there *is* still hope. You will know that He is for you and He loves you deeply, that you can turn to Him, and that He is your hope and expectation.

"I lift up my eyes to the hills. From where does my help come? My help comes from the LORD, who made heaven and earth" (ESV, Psalm 121:1–2).

Look up. Lift your eyes to the One who is able. Lift your eyes to your hope and expectation.

Application Questions

1. Can there always be hope in every situation you walk through? Do you hope in the outcome or do you hope in the One who is able?
2. What Scriptures can you find now that will help you when you walk in the midst of what seems like hopeless situations?
3. What do you believe will happen when you begin declaring these Scriptures over your circumstance?
4. As you declare hope or think about this hope, what do you see with your spiritual eyes?

CHAPTER 6

Truth Contrary to Our Experience

I remember coming home from the Mayo Clinic after Ronnie's surgery and talking to our children about what had happened. I will never forget our son Daniel's response.

"God can heal a cold, so of course, He can heal Dad."

His faith was so simple, so complete. Daniel, even though he was only 15, put this sickness and disease into perspective—God's perspective. To him, there was no other truth. God heals, so of course, his dad would be healed.

That is how we lived in those days of settling back into our life. There was no need to talk about it because it had already been resolved—Ronnie was healed by the stripes of Jesus (Isaiah 53:5).

One morning, as I sat before the Lord, I was led to Psalm 44. As I read this chapter, specifically verses 2 and 3, I heard the Lord whispering to my heart that I was to blow the trumpet of God over Ronnie and command the enemy cells to flee, and the army of God cells to arise and take back the land in a victory.

My first thought was, "Will Ronnie accept me doing this over him?"

My second thought was, "Wow, I wonder how I will make a bugle sound."

I knew that I needed to be obedient to what God was showing me, so I brought it up to Ronnie. To my amazement, he was in total agreement with me blowing the trumpet and declaring the Word over him. So every morning before he would go to work I would place my hand on his abdomen and blow the bugle, proclaiming what the Lord was showing me. Some days, the healing power of Jesus would fall so heavy that we would both be sweating, and Ronnie would have to change his shirt before leaving for work. We knew that our obedience to what Jesus was showing us was doing a work within his body.

Every morning the Holy Spirit would speak to me through Scripture and give me hope for our day. Nothing changed in the physical realm. We didn't see anything in the natural world. We knew that there was healing coming, and in the spiritual realm, Ronnie was getting stronger and stronger every day. We stayed in supernatural, unexplainable peace. From the outside, people would never have known what the doctors had told us.

One Friday, on my way to prayer at Kate's house, I sang worship songs and talked to the Lord about how I was walking through this with Him. I told Him how it felt like I must be losing it because I was filled with so much peace as I trusted His Word over our circumstances.

At the end of prayer that day, Kate said she had a Word for me from the Lord. She said she was sorry that it wasn't what she considered a powerful word for what I might need during this time. She went on to tell me that she saw me on the floor playing marbles, and the Lord wanted me to know that I wasn't losing my marbles.

I was so excited. Only I knew what that meant. She didn't have any idea about my conversation with the Lord in the car on my way over. But God did. He heard my heart and wanted me to know that I wasn't denying our circumstances; I was believing Him over them.

Trusting and believing God's Word as your truth can be contrary to the world you are walking in. This is what walking in His truth looks like: our circumstances may not confirm His truth; His truth changes our circumstances.

As the Bride of Christ, what we believe in our heart and put our trust in needs to be what He has said. We may have had other loves in the past and done things their way, but now we are His and His alone. These other loves are things that we have put before His truth. They are of this world and do not have the power to bring us peace and victory in our circumstances. Until we gave ourselves to Him, we used these other loves to dictate how we believed, made our decisions, and moved through our circumstances.

> His truth changes our circumstances

Now we trust only in Jesus, and the way we used to think is not to be mixed with His truth. We are to be transformed by the renewing of our mind and lay down what we believed before in exchange for His truth. There is no mixing of truths, for when we mix them we have diluted the power and strength of what He says, and it can lead us to being tossed about by the wind, to and fro, so that we end up not believing anything and completely confused.

Then we wonder why the truths of Jesus are not working in our lives. When we trust in a little of Jesus and His Word, a little of the world, a little from our emotions, a little from what the doctors may say, or what our friends say we should do, we can't expect victory.

One of my clients discovered the freedom and peace she received from trusting Jesus in her situation. She told me how it seemed crazy that she could walk in peace during one of the toughest trials of her life. She felt like she was losing it. If she stopped and analyzed the situation, thinking about her situation with her natural mind, she would fall back into fear. She discovered how she couldn't talk to her friends about the situation because they would give her their advice and that just dragged her back down again. As long as she kept her eyes on Jesus and trusted Him, and didn't look at what her feelings or her reasoning mind were telling her, she did great. She didn't go around and around about the situation in her thoughts, but stayed in peace, and was able to keep moving forward and not get tangled up in the circumstances.

Jesus' truth keeps us steady—keeps us moving forward instead of being frozen in fear. Keep your eyes on Him.

> Jesus' truth keeps us steady instead of being frozen in fear.

In the book of Matthew chapter 14, we can read about Peter's experience walking on water with Jesus. When the disciples saw Jesus walking on the sea, they were terrified and declared it was a ghost. But Jesus called out to them telling them it was Him, "I Am." Peter responded by asking Jesus to command him to come to Him if it was really Him. Jesus called Peter out onto the water, and so Peter climbed out of the boat and walked toward Jesus (Matthew 14:25–29).

When Jesus called Peter, he came right out. He believed the great I Am. Peter's eyes were on Jesus, and he believed who Jesus said He was. For him, the great I Am could do anything. This was God, and in Peter's heart, he probably remembered all that God had done for His people. He parted the Red Sea, He brought Daniel out of the lion's den, alive. What was walking on water? Nothing.

"But when he perceived and felt the strong wind, he was frightened and as he began to sink, he cried out, Lord save me [from death]!" (Matthew 14:30 AMPC)

It was when Peter felt what was going on in the natural realm that he became afraid and started sinking. When Peter had his eyes on the spiritual realm, ignoring the wind, waves, and natural law that man can't walk on water, he was able to walk out on the sea to Jesus. Peter agreed with a spiritual law that Jesus can do anything, and His Word is greater than our reality. He agreed with Jesus' word to "come." When Peter took his eyes off the truth and focused on the things of this natural world, using his reasoning mind, he could no longer reason his ability to walk on water with Jesus. Peter was frightened and began to sink.

In our situation, believing for Ronnie's healing, he would continually be reminded of what was going on in his body. He would have a pain in his abdomen, he would be more tired, and food wouldn't always sit right in his stomach. The enemy bombarded him with thoughts about what the doctors said. We had to stay steady and not have our eyes or thoughts turn to these things but keep our eyes on Jesus' Word and His truth. If we had given these symptoms attention, staying in faith would have been very difficult, if not impossible.

One day I went out for my morning run after blowing the trumpet over his body. I always run in the morning because I never get a side ache, whereas I almost always get a side ache when running later in the day. This particular morning, I hadn't been out for even a mile when my side started hurting. As I rounded back to cross our street and head on my typical path, I looked up and saw Ronnie driving to work. As I saw him, my side hurt even more. For the rest of the run, I prayed over Ronnie's body, believing that the Lord was showing me that it was Ronnie's side that was hurting. That afternoon when he called me from work, I asked him how he was doing. He said that his side had started hurting him on the way to work and that he had prayed and declared God's truth over his body during the drive. The pain had begun to subside by the time he pulled into the parking lot.

I shared with Ronnie what had happened to me and how the Lord had shown me to pray. I marveled at how good God was to bring us in unity and to show me how lying symptoms were coming against Ronnie.

If I had been thinking of my pain in the natural, I would have missed out on what God was showing me and would have missed being a part of Ronnie receiving relief and strength from the Lord. Believing and trusting Jesus doesn't make sense from our natural perspective. Our natural world is inferior to the spiritual world that we live in as His Bride.

Ephesians is one of my favorite books of the Bible. It speaks of the Lord's love for us and shows us who we are in Him.

Ephesians 2:4–7 states, "But God, being [so very] rich in mercy, because of His great *and* wonderful love with which He loved us, even when we were [spiritually] dead *and* separated from Him because of our sins, He made us [spiritually] alive together with Christ (for by His grace—His undeserved favor and mercy—you have been saved from God's judgment). And He raised us up together with Him [when we believed], and seated us with Him in the heavenly *places*, [because we are] in Christ Jesus, [and He did this] so that in the ages to come He might [clearly] show the immeasurable *and* unsurpassed riches of His grace in [His] kindness toward us in Christ Jesus [by providing for our redemption]."

We have been raised with Christ and are seated with Him in the heavenly places. As we walk through our present circumstances and take Him at His Word and know who we are in Him, we live out of a much higher place, a higher truth than the things of this world. The beauty of this position is that it was given to us—we don't have to earn it.

As His Bride, leave all your other loves behind. Leave the ways that you handled your circumstances behind and keep your eyes only on Him. Seek Him and His truth above all other thoughts that would lift themselves up as truth. His is the only truth, and everything else will fail you, leaving you as a scorned lover, deceived and hurt. Embrace the depth of His love for you in the midst of your circumstances. Receive Him. Invite Him in to release truth into everything you may be walking through right now. He will never leave you, He will never forsake you, and you will never be shamed for trusting Him.

Journal Entries

8/3/12

Blowing the army bugle over Ronnie, calling to attention every cell, strength to every cell that is part of the army of God and every cell of the enemy that has infiltrated into God's camp commanded to go, and vacated by the enemy in Jesus' name.

Psalm 44:2. God drove out the nations by His hand, and it was God's power that gave Israel a home by rooting out the heathen peoples, but Israel You spread out! Hallelujah!

Psalm 44:3. You did it, Lord. They didn't do it by sword or their own strength but Your right hand and Your arm and the light of Your countenance because You were favorable toward and did delight in them!

8/8/12

I praise You and I thank You, Lord. You are the One who is able to turn every hopeless situation around, You are able, You are willing. You are faithful and You also complete all that You begin. Lord, I thank You for completing the work You have begun in me and completing the work You have begun in Ronnie, Ben, Daniel, and Lydia. Burn within me, Lord, a holy passion for Your presence, for Your truth, for Your Word. Burn within Your Bride, for You are our Beloved and Your heart burns with passion for us.

Romans 8:11. God's Spirit in us raises us to life in our mortal body while on earth so that every dead place within us, within Ronnie, will be raised to life. Every cell that is from the enemy will die and every cell from the army of God will be raised to life, health, fullness of life! Hallelujah, glory to God!

8/15/12

Faith expects a good report. The expectation of good report receives a good report, expectation of good receives good. Lying symptoms came at Ronnie yesterday. I had a side ache when running and the Lord told me they were lying symptoms, and I was to come against them with the truth of the Word, and they left. Thank you, Jesus.

8/20/12

"We will overcome by the blood of the lamb and the word of our testimony."

I woke at 2 AM with these words rolling from my mind, my heart, my spirit. Yes, Lord, by Your blood, and with us agreeing with Your blood and truth, we will overcome! Hallelujah. I started praying in tongues, and the Lord said, "I am putting a covering over you and Ronnie, My Spirit will cover you, hover over you, because I want to talk with you, I have something to tell you." The presence and peace were mighty, and I fell asleep. I know He spoke into my spirit and I will hear—know—what He is telling me!

"I believe and therefore I have spoken" (2 Corinthians 4:13). Our faith is our profession, not just a confession, but may it move to a profession.

Hebrews 10:23. Let us hold fast the profession of our faith without wavering; (for He is faithful that promised), professing our promises because Jesus is faithful, and all the promises of God are yes and amen in Jesus. Hallelujah! We don't fight for faith, we search the Scriptures, eat on the Word until what we see is truth. It is deep within us, so when storms arrive it is what we believe. What we see by revelation is what we believe. We no longer fight but rest in the truth of who God is and what His Word says. He fights our battle, and we rest in Him knowing victory is ours!

Application Questions

1. What victory do you need in your life and your present circumstances?
2. What things in your life do not line up with the truth of the Word?
3. What Scripture can you begin declaring over your circumstance?
4. What things of this world, thoughts, beliefs, etc. do you need to let go of so that you are lined up with the truth of the Word?
5. Have you experienced what Peter did? Have you begun walking out in faith only to be overcome by the things of this world, which then caused you to reason away what God was telling you?
6. What can you learn from this experience that will prepare you the next time Jesus calls you to step out

of the boat, out of your understanding, and trust
His Word?

7. Who can you share this with to help you remain
   accountable to this paradigm shift in your thinking
   and belief system?

CHAPTER 7

Praise Brings us into His Glory

Your love is devoted like a ring of solid gold,
Like a vow that is tested, like a covenant of old.
Your love is enduring through the winter rain,
And beyond the horizon with mercy for today.

Faithful You have been and faithful You will be;
You pledge Yourself to me, and it's why I sing.

Your praise will ever be on my lips, ever be on my lips.
Your praise will ever be on my lips, ever be on my lips.
Your praise will ever be on my lips, ever be on my lips.
Your praise will ever be on my lips, ever be on my lips.

You Father the orphan;
Your kindness makes us whole.
And You shoulder our weakness,
And Your strength becomes our own.

Now you're making me like You,
Clothing me in white,
Bringing beauty from ashes,
For You will have Your Bride:

Free of all her guilt, and rid of all her shame,
And known by her true name, and it's why I sing.

Your praise will ever be on my lips, ever be on my lips.
Your praise will ever be on my lips, ever be on my lips.
Your praise will ever be on my lips, ever be on my lips.
Your praise will ever be on my lips, ever be on my lips.

You will be praised, You will be praised,
With angels and saints, we sing worthy are You Lord.
You will be praised, You will be praised,
With angels and saints, we sing worthy are You Lord.[1]

This is such a beautiful song that reveals clearly the reason for our praise. The Lord is worthy of praise. Not only because of the blessings we walk in or for the answers to our prayers, but rather, He is worthy to be praised for both times—on the days when everything turns out right and the days when nothing seems to go right. He is worthy to be praised because of who He is and all that He has already done for us on the cross. Our eternal salvation from the hands of the enemy is the most amazing miracle that He could ever do. For this, He is worthy of praise. So even on our worst day, we have reasons to praise Him and lift high His holy name.

On Sunday mornings we worship together as fellow believers, and we sing how worthy God is of our praise. What happens to our thoughts of His worthiness in the midst of our struggles? I have learned that it is one thing to discuss how worthy God is of praise, and quite another to discover how praise in the midst of difficulty can change everything.

Before Ronnie's sickness, two times in my life stand out when I think about the power of praise. I experienced how praising the Lord during storms is a powerful weapon for my thoughts and that it allows me to walk in peace and victory no matter the situation.

As I have shared in previous chapters, prior to Ronnie's illness I experienced multiple miscarriages that deeply hurt my heart. That hurt attached itself to the pain that was not healed from my abortion. In 2002, after two miscarriages, Ronnie and I were thrilled to know that I was pregnant again. The doctors monitored me very closely; in fact, I had an ultrasound every week. The focus on the baby and the baby's development kept my eyes directly there. I was so thankful that we were going to have a baby, but it was very easy for fear to creep in because of my previous miscarriages and brokenness.

One morning when I was about three months along, I began spotting. This doesn't necessarily mean something is wrong; it can be quite normal for some pregnancies. I had never experienced this in my other pregnancies unless something was wrong, so I began spiraling into the winds of fear and what-ifs. I sat down on the couch and knew that I had to quiet myself before the Lord. I had called the doctor, but they could not see me for several hours. I could feel the roller coaster beginning, and from all of my roller coaster rides in the past, I knew where they were going to take me—right into the arms of fear until my world raged out of control. I had to grab hold of Jesus, and I had to do it fast.

I remember sitting on the couch and turning my thoughts toward Jesus. I recalled all that He had done for me. He saved me. He redeemed me. He loved me long before I knew how to love Him. As I turned my thoughts to the beauty of who He was, peace came and wrapped its arms around me, around my heart. The thoughts of fear became fewer and fewer. I sank into the arms of the Lord and told Him I trusted Him with this baby. He gave this baby to me, and I trusted Him to see us through. This would have been an impossible thought over a year ago—before He healed my heart from my abortion. I was learning to trust Him because He was good and only had good things for me.

When we have something heavy on our heart, we can take it to the Lord in our prayer time and end up spending the whole time of prayer talking to the Lord about the problem. Every time that I have done that, I have gotten up from my prayer time still carrying the burden in my heart. I have learned to bring my concern to the Lord, lay it at His feet, and then begin to praise Him that He has taken care of it. Only then can I get up from my time of prayer with my heart free of the burden and full of an expectation of Him taking care of it for me. We don't have to beg the Lord to take our burden or for Him to handle it for us. We need only ask and begin praising Him for what He will do because He has already done it at the cross.

We all know what a miracle it is to be in perfect peace through a tsunami of emotions and fear.

Jesus is peace. Jesus is perfect peace. He cannot be anything else. It is not that He is able to bring peace, it is that *He* is peace. When we don't feel peace, we agree with someone other than Jesus. When I began to praise the Lord for all He had done for me, I experienced His peace like a flood. I will never forget that morning I told Him I could trust Him with my pregnancy because I had experienced everything but His peace with my recent pregnancies. This was a miracle. A miracle that came through praise.

The other monumental moment in my life that praise changed everything was when Ronnie had the opportunity to move us to North Carolina through a transfer with the company. It was my dream to live in North Carolina. I could tell you all the reasons why we should have lived there. Ronnie was very hesitant to take the position, but he finally said yes. I was elated. He was crushed.

He said yes on a Friday, but by Monday morning he couldn't continue in that direction and brought every preparation for the move to a grinding halt. I was devastated. In fact, that probably isn't even a good picture of what was going on in my heart. I was so incredibly disappointed in the decision and what I thought that meant for my life that I couldn't even interact with him before he went to work.

I spent my day crying and feeling sorry for myself, even telling myself that I only had to survive 40 more years in Iowa, and then I would be in paradise. So it was only a matter of figuring out how to be happy here for 40 or so more years. It sounds laughable now, but that was how far my sight had sunk. That was how much I had based my happiness upon the move.

By the end of the day, I thought I had gotten to the point that I could deal with my disappointment. I figured that in my sorry state the best I could ever do about what I was feeling was find ways to deal with it. Oh yes, it would always be there—the feeling that I would love to be living somewhere else, and the knowledge that it was my husband's choice to stay. It would be my cross to bear, but I could do it. I would white-knuckle it through. I had made this so big in my heart that I didn't think anything God could tell me would take it away.

When Ronnie came home from work and I saw his face, all I could do was make underhanded comments about what he had done and how I felt about it. All through dinner, I was rotten and selfish. Bitterness was attempting to take root in my heart. I hated feeling this way but had no idea how I was going to be free from this. I assumed the only way it would be better was time—time and the sacrifice of my dreams.

After dinner, I was to meet my friends Kate and Jane to pray over Jane's new office building for their business. We were going to pray and anoint the building with oil. I knew that my heart was not right, but I just wanted out of the house. I went to the office to personally tell them that my heart did not have the right attitude to join them in prayer. When I told them where my heart was, my friends looked at me and said, "You are not leaving." Kate began walking around the reception area singing praises. She led us in singing every praise song she could remember and told me to join with them.

I suppose you could say I joined in.

Kate and Jane were singing. All I could do was mouth the words, with my head down and my hands clenched at my side.

Kate and Jane continued singing praises to the Lord. I began saying the words along with them, my head slowly raising up from looking at the floor.

My friends sang and sang from their hearts. I begrudgingly sang the words, my unclenched fists now hanging at my side.

They raised their hands, praising Jesus. As the praises came from my lips, my heart began to soften. I started singing from my heart the praises of our King, with my arms raised to worship.

It was like a crack opened up in my stone cold, hard heart, and a song was whispered. As I sang more and more (Kate knew enough songs to keep going for hours), the crack burst open, the hardness of my heart fell off, and I was open again to the stirring of the Lord—open again to sing His song.

A miracle took place. I couldn't keep my heart from wanting to sing. As they sang another song and I followed their lead, my heart softened, and my eyes turned to the Lord. My heart sang those words, and I slowly sang with all that I had in me. I knew that if I stopped then, nothing had changed yet in my heart except that I was positioning myself to receive. So we just kept on singing.

After about an hour of singing, Kate and Jane came over and began praying over me. The presence of the Lord came and ushered in His glory. I felt Jesus' loving arms around me. All I could do was weep. Jesus reached in and took my pain, my disappointment, my bitterness out of my heart. He carried it away from me. I could feel the burden, the heaviness, lifting off me. I was free. It was a tangible experience of the Lord's presence. My original emotional state didn't keep Him from coming. He came and changed everything for me because I positioned my heart to receive.

There is healing in the glory of the Lord. 2 Corinthians 3:18 says that we are transformed from glory to glory by being in His presence.

My soul was transformed.

My thoughts were transformed.

My mind was transformed.

My will was transformed.

My emotions were transformed.

After Kate and Jane had prayed over me, we finished up our time together by praying over the building. I was elated. I was set free. I easily prayed and believed, and decreed over the business all the plans that the Lord was showing us in our hearts.

I went home that night and found Ronnie getting ready for bed. He didn't quite know how to interact with me because of the way I had left. I looked straight into his eyes and told him I was sorry. I said that I had let go of the hurt in my heart for the way things had turned out. I would not bring this up again in our marriage. It was finished, and the Lord had healed my heart through praising Him and bringing in His glory. It was a miracle.

Even as I shared this with him, I was amazed at my words and what I was able to feel in my heart. I didn't have to carry this inside and try to deal with it. I wasn't giving up my dream of living somewhere else. I was grabbing hold of Jesus and all that He had for us. I knew that what He had for us was so much better than what I had been pushing upon my husband.

Through worshipping the Lord with my friends, we ushered in His very presence, and I was able to participate in the great exchange. I would not have found myself at this place as quickly if it had not been for my friends helping to press in for more and usher in His presence, which carried with it His glory.

As His Bride, we are united in Him, and the great exchange of the cross is always ours. At the cross, He took our sin, judgment, shame, sickness, poverty, and pain and gave us forgiveness, righteousness, life, glory, healing, prosperity, and joy. As we praise and worship Him, we let go of the things in our heart and our hands and receive from Him all that He has already done.

I share my past experiences because they were monumental in my life and helped me to understand the power of praise and what happens in my heart when I worship the One who is worthy. My mind can't wrap around how this happens, but I don't have to understand—I just need to believe and receive. A reasoning mind would keep what He has for me far away. The world would have told me that my resentment towards my husband for the change in plans was justified, and it would take a while for me to work through it and get past it. I may even have to live with that disappointment in my heart forever.

Jesus told me otherwise. Jesus gave me a miracle.

In *Making the Most of Your Meltdowns,*[2] Brenda Thomas discusses how, when we are facing difficult situations, our attitude determines our altitude. If we're whining, complaining and murmuring, it won't get us very far. But rejoicing always brings God on the scene. There comes a time when you have to lift Your hands. You have to shout unto the Lord. You may even need to dance or spin around. You have to do whatever it takes to release the joy of the Lord on the inside of you to shake off depression and oppression. Joy will restore, and it will make things better than before. God doesn't just give back what the enemy stole. He gives all that back plus even more, added and multiplied unto you. You can't beat a joyful believer.

Years later, as we walked through Ronnie's illness, hearing all that the doctors had to say, we knew that praise would change our heart and help us to stay on the path that the Lord had for us. Praise would position us to receive healing, strength, peace, and joy.

Praise is a position. A position that places us ready to receive. A position that helps us see with eyes of faith and not look at our circumstances with a reasoning mind.

With every word that the doctor gave us about Ronnie's impending death, we praised the Lord that His truth was greater than any man's opinions and statistics. We turned our eyes and thoughts from what was said and placed them on the Lord and what He had already done for us on the cross.

We praised Jesus that though Ronnie's body wasn't manifesting it yet, he was healed. Jesus healed him. The bracelet I wore on my wrist carried the words of Jesus from Luke 8:50, "Simply Believe."

After Ronnie's first chemo treatment in late August, he didn't feel that bad. He was able to continue working and watch what he ate for his nausea. We went to the lake a week after the treatment for a Labor Day celebration. We enjoyed a wonderful weekend together. We don't have internet or cable at the lake for a good reason. We spend our time together as a family, enjoying one another's company.

On Monday, when Ronnie woke up he felt like he was getting a fever and laid low that morning. We had lunch and then headed home in the early afternoon. Ronnie wasn't feeling any better, so I helped the boys get everything put away, turned off, and locked up. We loaded up the car and headed home.

When we arrived, Ronnie was able to take his temperature and found it over 100 °F and climbing. We knew that any increased temperature after his chemo treatment should be taken very seriously, so we went right to the hospital.

I called Kate to rally the prayer warriors in praying for this fever and any infection to be gone. At the ER they did several tests, took lots of blood. God was so good that the fever, which had reached 104 °F, was below 100 °F by the time they admitted him. The initial results showed an infection, but the exact type would take several days to be cultured. It was close to midnight by the time Ronnie was wheeled to his room, so I got him settled and went home to the kids. I knew that Jesus had this for Ronnie, and he would be discharged from the hospital to come home soon. Fear and thoughts of dread attempted to grab hold of my heart, but I turned to praising God for who He was in the midst of these new symptoms.

While Ronnie was in the hospital, he was given a powerful antibiotic intravenously to help stop the infection. His fever never returned after it left him on Monday night when he was admitted. The nurses continued to monitor his temperature, amazed at his progress.

We talked with the doctor, and he knew that we had plans to go to Ankeny to be part of a healing ministry's weekend conference. We had been planning our trip for weeks and were very excited that this ministry was coming to Iowa. The timing was amazing. The doctor and nurses continued to tell us how sick Ronnie was, even though there were no physical signs.

Were there moments that our thoughts went to the what-ifs? Yes.

Were there moments that fear and dread tried to trap us with a vision of death? Yes.

It wasn't that those thoughts didn't come, but it was what we did about them that mattered.

Praise and thankfulness kept our hearts full. Coming into the Lord's presence changed everything for us. He became bigger. Our hearts knew He was able to heal. He is always able. We knew that He was good and had good plans for us. So, did the thoughts come? Yes, but we didn't agree with them. Praise wouldn't let us.

Praise is not a place that you enter in order to get what you want. Praise is a position before the Lord. Our desire was to be in the Lord's presence.

Psalm 16:11 says that God will make known the path of life for us, and in His presence, we will receive the fullness of joy and in His right hand are pleasures forevermore.

Fear and dread do not reside where truth and peace reign. Ronnie and I didn't want to experience the road of fear; we wanted to experience the fullness of joy that only God could bring us. That fullness of joy is not based upon our circumstances but upon where we live and who lives inside of us.

Ronnie ended up coming home from the hospital after just three days. His blood work showed he had an infection in his blood stream. We didn't fully understand the extent of it until we had a follow-up doctor visit before we left town the next week. The doctor shared that patients with this condition stay in the hospital for at least a week and that this particular blood infection has a high death rate. Praise God—Ronnie was out in three days with no more fever. It was a miracle.

The antibiotic that he had to continue taking during our trip to the conference was so strong that it made him feel like his skin was crawling and his insides were waiting to bust free. It was a continual struggle to keep his mind off what his body was feeling. As we worshiped and praised the Lord, his body came into peace, and he could sit and receive from the ministry.

We were so blessed by the conference we attended, and Ronnie received an impartation of healing through personal prayer and ministry from the anointed man of God who was leading the conference. We knew that God had blessed us and made a way for us to be at the conference to receive all that He had prepared to give to Ronnie. The ministry blessed Ronnie so much that he began talking about all that God had before him in his life—how God was helping him to see his life with eyes of faith, and how he looked forward to ministering to others the truth of Jesus and His grace.

Our praise positioned us to receive. Our praise positioned us to see with eyes of faith, hope, and expectation. Our praise to the One who is worthy kept our eyes above our circumstances to the place where we are seated with Him in Heavenly places. Our praise brought us into His presence, and we found that nothing we were holding onto was as wonderful as the pleasures He had for us at His right hand. It wasn't hard to open up our hands and receive all that He had for us. We didn't want to keep our hands closed. Praise that brings us into His presence changes everything and gives us the peace that passes all understanding.

Journal Entries

8/16/12

I love starting new journals. It's like a stepping stone into the deeper things of God. This journal is starting with a new school year and walking into great depths of the manifestations of healing in Ronnie's body, an awakening to our destiny, and being transformed in ways and depths I could never have imagined. Our ride with God is never boring, only amazing and better than we could hope for. I can't wait to experience all that God has for us in the coming days. Hallelujah, there is great victory and rejoicing in the camp of the righteous! Psalm 119:9–12; Daniel 5:11–12.

"Blessed are those who dwell in Your house and Your presence; they will be singing Your praises all the day long. Selah!" (Psalm 84:4) Oh Lord, may I dwell in Your house, Your presence always, and may praise be upon my lips flowing from my heart all the day long. Praise and Your presence go hand in hand. As I remain in praise, I remain in Your presence. Fear, torment, disease, frustration, anger, confusion cannot come near me to move me out of Your presence!

Psalm 18:28–50—Word of the Lord today to speak over Ronnie as I blow the bugle and call the troops of the army of God to attend to the cells of his body. God's Word does not return void but accomplishes all that it was sent to do; He watches over His Word to perform it, for He is faithful and true forever. Selah!

8/24/12

Praise You, Lord Jesus. I am in awe of You. I praise Your Holy name and trust in You and You alone. Some trust in princes and other false gods that attempt to exalt themselves above You. But I trust in my God who is the only God, my Deliverer, Strong Tower, Savior, Lord over all! I trust in You and You alone at all times. You are my Savior. Bless the Lord, oh my soul, and all that is in me bless His Holy name. Bless the Lord, oh my soul, and forget not all His benefits, who forgives all my iniquities, heals all of my diseases, and redeems my life from the pit. Bless the Lord, oh my soul!

Ephesians 3:16–19. Spirit, soul, and body, I receive all of You today, Lord, and all You have for me in the rich treasury of Your storehouses in Heaven. Come and fill me completely, flood me with Your very presence that You would make Your permanent home in me, sustaining me and quickening me to life—every part of me.

Romans 8:11. Spirit which dwells in me, You raised up Jesus from dead and will also restore to life my mortal body!

Proverbs 4:22. Attend to the Word, for it is healing and health to all my flesh! Faith that works is built on hope that is rooted in the heart, declared by the mouth, and demonstrated with the corresponding action.

1 John 5:4. We have victory in every area of our life because we are born of God and have faith—overcoming faith! We have victory over our health, in our marriage, in our finances, for our children, in our relationships, and in our workplace. We have victory! Glory to God. Hallelujah! As I trust in You, Lord, and not in my own understanding, but acknowledging You, You will make my path straight to Victory!

Application Questions

1. What does praise help lift you out of?
2. How can praise change your present circumstances?
3. Do you have friends or other believers that you can confide in to help you turn your eyes to Jesus when you need help and cannot praise Him on your own?
4. How do you see the power of praise changing difficult circumstances you may walk through in the future?
5. Do you find it difficult to enter into praise? If praising Jesus out loud is a new concept for you, try reading the Psalms out loud in your quiet time with the Lord. As you read them out loud, envision yourself speaking these Psalms before the throne of God. Continue this practice daily and insert your own personal praises into the Psalms. Thank the Lord that He is giving you a heart to worship Him.

CHAPTER 8

Peace, the Anchor for Our Soul

As I shared in the previous chapters, Ronnie and I walked in peace that we could not understand. Held in the bubble of God's grace that carried us through, we believed continually in Ronnie's healing.

The months that followed our experience at the healing conference were a time of miracles. Ronnie came home and experienced strength and health. Because of the infection that he received from the chemo treatment, his oncologist suggested he take a break from the chemo, and Ronnie decided that he would not go through it again. The doctors were hoping the chemo would prolong his life but were not expecting it to provide a cure. The quality of life that the chemo gave Ronnie was not worth it to him.

Ronnie continued to work full-time and chose not to travel until his health improved. Before his diagnosis, Ronnie was traveling every week for at least two days and usually more.

We had no doubt that he would get better. Our faith was completely resting on the Lord's truth and His healing that he gave us at the cross. Friends covered us with prayer. We also had prayer times together at our house. It was a beautiful time of going before the Lord and sitting in His presence.

We attended the conference in September, and his health remained the same until the end of November. His body wasn't able to rest at night, and the long sleepless nights wore him out physically. Spiritually, he was stronger than ever. We kept pressing on. We never talked about anything but healing coming his way. The family interaction each evening was exactly as it had always been. This to us was peace. This to us was believing in the One who heals.

It was in the first part of December that Ronnie began not feeling well. He wanted to see the doctor and check in with him. The doctor ordered a scan, and shortly after, more symptoms came. It truly was a miracle that even though the scan showed growths in his liver, Ronnie was not jaundiced. Ronnie started retaining some fluid the next week, so we scheduled an appointment to remove some of it. Ronnie was still working at this time, and it was getting close to the company's two-week break over the holidays. We were thankful that he would have this time to rest and not have the stress of his work.

I do not have the words to express the peace that we lived in. We were solid in our belief that healing was coming. Neither fear nor discussion of death was ever a part of our daily lives. Our lives went on as normal. Ronnie was at complete peace with the Lord, not begging for his healing but simply believing.

I continued mentoring several girls from our church. It is one of the things I love to do for the Lord. I think I am more blessed from these times together than they are. One day, when the girls came over, they walked in and said that our house was full of peace. They could feel it the moment they walked through the door. We felt it because it was where our heart resided, but it was a blessing to hear that when others came to our home, they too experienced His peace.

Christmas came, and our two boys went to my parents' house for the traditional Christmas Eve festivities. Ronnie felt more comfortable being in his own bed and at home. So the boys went, and Lydia and I stayed home with Ronnie. A friend of mine wanted to help me prepare Christmas dinner so that I could spend time with everyone and not worry about the food. The boys came home Christmas morning, and our friend Luana came with a feast for our meal. Then we prepared the house for Ronnie's mom to come over for an early dinner. During our time together as a family, Ronnie was up and about, taking care of his mom and getting chairs where they needed to be. You would have never known that he wasn't feeling well.

That night, after his mom went back to her assisted living apartment, we invited friends to come over and be with us. Ronnie rested on the sofa, and the rest of us laughed and enjoyed each other's company. Ronnie enjoyed having people in our home even though he was tired and relaxing in the other room.

We continued our times of prayer with our friends. Several of those times stand out to me as miraculous times in the Lord's presence. Each time we talked afterward, everyone shared how they felt the presence of angels and the heavy presence of the Lord. I believe that is why our home and our hearts filled with peace. Our desire was to be in His presence and to enter into all that He is and has for us.

The night of December 27, 2012, was a night of miracles, a night when Heaven entered our home. Kate and Tom came over to pray with Ronnie and me. The kids were already in bed, so it was later in the evening. This was the first day that Ronnie stayed in our bed all day and did not come downstairs to the family room. Kate and Tom came and prayed with Ronnie and me in our room. We began singing songs. We would make up words to the songs. Ronnie loved it, and even though he was tired, he sang the Amen portion of the song. We would sing, "Ronnie's being healed now," and then he would join us singing, "Amen." It was such a blessing to see him at peace and singing.

We began praying after our praising. Heaven was tangible. As we had our eyes closed, I remember seeing in my spirit a small angel coming with a silver tray with containers on it.

Silently, I asked the Lord if we were to have communion together and I heard His response in my heart, "No, she is bringing medicine for Ronnie."

At that exact moment, I heard Kate say, "Ronnie, I am going to read from the Word of God for it is medicine to our bodies."

I knew at that moment that the four of us were one in the Spirit and engaging Heaven in our time of prayer.

After Kate had read from the Word, we each prayed what was laid on our heart for Ronnie, believing and declaring his healing. We all kept our eyes closed. We knew the room was full of angels.

I saw with my spiritual eyes another angel come and rest by Ronnie's head on the bed where the other angel had already been sitting and caring for Ronnie. This angel was also smaller, almost like a child. She administered cloths to Ronnie's head, caring for his physical body. The love with which they cared for Ronnie was beautiful.

When Ronnie fell asleep, the three of us left the room and went downstairs. We were each bursting to share what we had seen with our spiritual eyes. None of us had wanted to open our eyes because the presence of angels and Heaven had filled our bedroom and we were all hesitant to open and look. We wanted to keep seeing in the spiritual realm and not miss anything.

Tom shared that he had seen Ronnie laying in our bed. He was well and had sat up, fully clothed in comfortable clothing. As he flung the covers off him, Ronnie had declared, "I am so glad this is all behind me. Let's go."

The three of us were elated. The expectancy we had for Ronnie's healing filled us with hope for what God was doing in his body. When we had left Ronnie upstairs he was not jaundiced, there was no fluid building up in his tissues, and he was resting comfortably. A miracle was taking place, and we felt complete peace.

The Scripture I wore on my wrist, Luke 8:50, was also told in Mark 5:36.

After Jairus' servant had come with bad news, "overhearing what was being said, Jesus said to the synagogue official, 'Do not be afraid; only keep on believing [in Me and my power].'"

This is what Ronnie and I did; we kept on believing in Jesus and His power no matter the news that was given us. Our lives were peaceful. Our thoughts were full of peace as we kept believing in Jesus. Circumstances and bad news did not sway us in believing. We had learned on this journey that all sorts of news would come our way. Most of it completely out of the blue, attempting to knock us off the foundation of Jesus. As we had walked these past months, we knew that news, reports, and statistics would only toss us back and forth, up and down, side to side. We chose not to go there. We chose not to keep our eyes and thoughts on the news. We chose to keep our eyes on Jesus, and the perfect peace that He promised was ours.

In our time of prayer, when we experienced Heaven, we could feel peace. Heaven was not surprised by any of Ronnie's symptoms. Heaven knows only peace. When I felt fear trying to creep in, I quieted myself in the Lord and envisioned myself seated next to Christ in the Heavenly realm. Peace overtook me. God is on His throne, Jesus is seated at His right hand, and we are seated next to Him because

> We are seated with Christ in the Heavenly realm where peace reigns.

God the Father raised us up in Him (Ephesians 2:6–7). That is our position now as we walk on this earth. Isn't it amazing? We are seated with Christ in the Heavenly realm where peace reigns. Fear has no place there. We can bring peace into every situation as we remain in our Heavenly place.

As I rested in His presence, I breathed in and began listening for His heart. I wanted to beat to the rhythm of His heart. When fear comes upon me, my heart starts racing, and my breathing becomes shallow and fast. Being in His presence changes all of that. We can tune our heart to the beating of His heart. We can look at fear from that position and tell fear it has no place here, tell unbelief it has no place here. As we walk in His peace, we bring Heaven to earth. We bring His kingdom into our situation, our home, and this earthly realm. Kingdom truth is much greater than natural reality. *Simply believe.*

As His Bride, Christ only asks us to believe in Him and on Him. Just as for Jairus, we don't have to do anything but believe. Everything we need, everything we desire, is for Jesus to handle. Ronnie and I didn't have to concern ourselves with how his healing would come in the midst of what the world said was impossible. Our responsibility was to believe.

I remember when Ronnie would come home after a tough day. I would remind him that we had pleased the Lord God Almighty that day because we had put our faith in Him. I would tell him that we had an amazing day because we had pleased our God. The only thing that can please God is our faith, and that is what we had done one day at a time (Hebrews

11:6). I remember how Ronnie would smile and laugh thinking about how great a blessing that was, to please his God.

"God's peace [shall be yours, the tranquil state of a soul assured of its salvation through Christ, and so *fearing nothing from God* and being content with its earthly lot of whatever sort that is, that peace] which transcends all understanding shall garrison and mount guard over your hearts and minds" (Philippians 4:7, italics mine).

Peace can be ours because we know God is good and has only good things for us. We can trust God and His plan and His ways, and fear nothing from Him. Come what may, He's got it for us. What we need is ours, and we are His. This is why it is so important to know that God is good and to know His love and goodness for us. It is impossible to lean on, trust, and hope in a God you do not know and do not believe has good things for you.

"For though the mountains should depart and the hills be shaken or removed, yet My love and kindness shall not depart from you, nor shall My covenant of peace and completeness be removed, says the Lord, Who has compassion on you" (Isaiah 54:10).

Peace is a foundational key that comes out of simply believing and trusting in the One who is able.

Journal Entries

11/9/12

Lord, You are so beautiful, loving, and wonderful. Your love draws me in, and causes a hunger for more of You. I want to know You more; in You is a peace and joy that I could never have outside or apart from You. In Your presence is joy. Oh Lord, I pray that joy bubbles up from within my belly today, joy because I have You, and nothing else can move me from that place of peace where joy bubbles up like a fountain.

11/25/12

Praise You, Lord. I worship You, Lord. In Your presence, I know everything is going to be okay. In Your presence is joy forevermore. In Your presence, I can see truth because darkness can't stay in Your presence.

Psalm 121. The Lord is my keeper. He keeps us in His hand, as we come in and go out. He keeps me from all evil and He keeps my life, for my life is in His hands. I will trust Him at all times. He delivers me. He keeps me. Praise You, Jesus. You keep Ronnie, Ben, Daniel, Lydia, myself, Mom and Dad, and Lori in Your hand. I praise You for Your love for me, for us. I praise You and set my sight on You and not my circumstances. You alone are God and You alone are good. My joy comes from You; my strength rises up from that joy. I will walk in joy as I walk through circumstances being strengthened by You and not moved, for I keep my eyes on You, Lord. This is a song that is bubbling up from within me: "I keep my eyes on You, Lord. You are the author of my faith. You are the One who keeps me straight. Your path is perfectly ordained, and You keep my feet walking straight. I will trust in You. I will trust in You. Your Word brings light to me. I will trust in You; I will trust in You; You are my Lord and my God. I will trust in You, and not by sight will I walk, but Your Word is my sight, Lord. Your Word is my truth, Lord."

12/4/12

I keep my eyes and heart fixed on You, Lord. As I pray with thanksgiving, lifting all of my requests to You, You will guard and garrison my heart and my mind to keep them in perfect peace. I thank You, Lord. You keep me. I praise You, Lord, You are the One I desire. You are the One I adore. It's You and only You, Lord. Praise You, Jesus. I love Your presence. Your presence is Heaven to me, Lord; everything changes and I receive a new perspective. I can see from a different point of view! Praise You, Lord Jesus, for Your love and mercy, Your grace and strength, for being my joy which is my strength. Holy Spirit whispered to go to Psalm 108. O God, my heart is filled (steadfast, in the confidence of faith); I will sing, yes I will sing praises, even with my glory. Awake, harp and lyre; I myself will wake very early—I will awaken the dawn! I will praise and give thanks to You, O Lord, among the peoples; and will sing praises unto You among the nations. For Your mercy and loving-kindness are great and high in the heavens. Your truth and faithfulness reach the skies. Be exalted, O God, above the heavens and let Your glory be over all the earth. I began singing this Psalm and worshipping Jesus. I heard Him say, "Agree with the Word. Nothing disagrees with the Word. Agree with the Word, align yourself with the Word, speak the Word over situations. It is the truth, it is the way, and it is the agreement of Heaven. Be sure there is life in the Word, mercy and grace in the Word, faith and obedience in the Word." Hallelujah. Thank You, Lord.

12/27/12

I come to sit with You today, Jesus. I need my Word from You. The Holy Spirit said to see Jesus high and lifted up, keep your eyes on Jesus. Word for my day today comes from Psalm 90:16. "Let Your work [the signs of Your power] be revealed to Your servants and Your [glorious] majesty to their children!" Hallelujah, Lord. Show us Your power.

Application Questions

1. What is robbing you of peace today?
2. How can you turn your eyes to the Lord and receive His peace?
3. What does peace look like for you?
4. What will you need to take your eyes off of to experience peace?
5. Have you ever experienced Jesus' peace in a situation that brought you no peace? If yes, as you look back at that experience, what did it feel like and what did you do to get there?

SECTION 3

The Bridal Chamber

At the end of the period of separation, the groom would come to take his bride to live with him. The taking of the bride usually occurred at night. The groom, best man, and other male escorts left the groom's father's house and conducted a torchlight procession to the home of the bride. Although the bride was expecting her groom to come for her, she did not know the exact time of his coming. As a result, the groom's arrival was preceded by a shout. This shout forewarned the bride to be prepared for the coming of the groom.

After the groom had received his bride, together with her female attendants, the enlarged wedding party returned from the bride's home to the groom's father's house. Upon arrival, the wedding party found the wedding guests already assembled.

Shortly after arrival, the bride and groom were escorted by the other members of the wedding party to the Bridal Chamber (*huppah*). Before entering the chamber, the bride remained veiled so that no one could see her face. While the groomsmen and bridesmaids waited outside, the bride and groom entered the Bridal Chamber alone. There in the privacy of that place, they entered into physical union for the first time, thereby consummating the marriage that had been covenanted months earlier.

After the marriage had been consummated, the groom announced the consummation to the other members of the wedding party waiting outside the chamber (John 3:29). These people passed on the news of the marital union to the wedding guests. Upon receiving this good news, the wedding guests feasted and made merry for the next seven days.

During the seven days of the wedding festivities, which were sometimes called "the seven days of the huppah," the bride remained hidden in the Bridal Chamber. At the conclusion of these seven days, the groom brought his bride out of the Bridal Chamber, now with her veil removed, so that all could see who his bride was[1].

104

In the intimacy of the Bridal Chamber, we can no longer hide. The veil is no longer over our face. The clothing that we have worn at our wedding is taken off. Everything is exposed to our lover, our Bridegroom. It is the place of intimacy where we become one with each other. Everything He has becomes ours, and everything we once were is taken off so that we can become all that He is.

As my life entered into this place with the Lord, all the things that I once knew to carry me through would no longer be adequate. Everything that I once believed in would no longer be enough. Everything that had filled my heart would no longer satisfy. All the things that I had used to survive would no longer give me strength. To be filled, completely satisfied, and able to keep moving forward, I would have to receive from Him. I learned in the time of preparation that He was safe, that I could trust Him. I knew it was safe to enter into the Bridal Chamber even though I was not fully aware of the layers that would soon have to come off to experience Him even more deeply than before. It was my desire for Him that arose out of my deep need for Him that led me to walk into this intimate place.

I had been learning how safe it was to be with Him and how, as I trusted Him above the ways of the world, I was okay, and I could rise above the storms that tried to drag me down, entangle my heart, and keep me swirling with no place to land. My spiritual perspective in the Bridal Chamber is always one of overcoming victory, whereas my natural perspective in this earthly realm can be defeat, loss, pain, and torment.

This was it. As I entered into the intimacy of this place, I was unsure of what would transpire there, but I knew that I would reemerge and be revealed as His own. The transformation would take place in areas where I didn't know I would need it, but He knew. As I entered in, I told Him that I was willing to take off everything that encumbered me so that I could be transformed into whom He said I was. He is such a gentleman that if I don't give Him permission, He will never overstep the boundary that I set. If I am not willing and ready to receive Him in a certain area of my life, then He waits for me to give Him permission, and in the meantime, I am unable to be transformed in that place. In the intimacy of the Bridal Chamber, I am giving Him full permission. I am not holding anything back.

In accordance with Jewish custom, the Bride does not come out of the Bridal Chamber until seven days have passed. Seven is the number of completion. We are invited to enter into the Bridal Chamber and experience our Bridegroom completing everything in us. He reveals us as His own, and we are then known by who we are—His Bride, that He died to give everything to, the passion of His heart. How beautiful and wonderful to know that as He transforms us, He reveals us. He not only reveals us to those around us, but He also reveals us to ourselves. We discover who He has called us to be. We walk out our true identity. When you are in the Bridal Chamber, and you look into His eyes, you see your true identity in the reflection. You may have seen a glimmer of yourself before you entered, but now you can see clearly. There is no distraction there. There is nothing but yourself to be seen in the reflection of His eyes. His love burns completely for you. His eyes don't see anything but you. You are His, and He is yours.

We know that our Bridegroom is coming to take His Bride. He is coming for a Bride who is clean and pure, and without spot or wrinkle (Ephesians 5:27). The beauty of our relationship with Jesus is that we can enter into the most intimate place with Him now. We do not have to wait until He returns to go into the Bridal Chamber with Him. Through our relationship with Him, we can enter in. We can dive into the depths of His love for us. He is passionate for you, and He is passionate for you to experience all that He has for you in the intimacy of His Bridal Chamber.

CHAPTER 9

The One We Trust

B eing in a place of expectation and hope is a beautiful, peaceful place to reside. As we stand believing in the Lord for His truth to come to pass, we remain hopeful and full of expectation. What do we do when what we believe for doesn't come to pass? Can we still hope? Can we still be filled full of hope and expectation?

I can imagine that as the Bride is waiting for her Bridegroom and getting prepared for the time he comes, there is excitement in the preparation. Each day she has thoughts of what it will be like to be with him. Each day she wonders if this is the day that he will come for her.

Then she hears the shout announcing the wedding party's arrival to take her away. Everything she has been hoping for will now be made known to her. As she rides with the Bridegroom to his father's home, to the place that he has made ready for her, I imagine her excited but scared, not knowing what lies ahead. She has been dreaming of this day, but now it is here. Will it be anything like what she thought it was going to be?

She ventures into the unknown, crosses over the Bridal Chamber threshold. She may not know what lies before her, but she knows she is to trust the one who has come for her. She belongs to her Bridegroom now, her husband. All of her time of preparation was for this moment. All for the time that she gives herself to him completely.

This is not the time to run away scared, frightened of the unknown. Your time before this moment was getting to know Jesus, getting to know the One you can now completely trust. Anything that you used to keep yourself hidden will soon be removed.

The outcomes, the circumstances, the needs, the emotions are all left at the threshold as He becomes the One thing. The desire for Him alone is what pulls us in. Praise upon our heart for all that He has done keeps our feet moving forward into the place He has prepared. Nothing else matters. This is everything to us now. No matter what this depth of relationship with Him entails or becomes, we are so overcome by His beauty that we enter in.

We know that it is not about our performance. In this intimate place, it is not about us and what we do or do not do. It is based completely upon Jesus' value of us, the price He paid for us. He gave everything for us to be able to enter in. Now we give everything to Him to be able to be with Him.

Before I entered into this place with Him, I would have told you that I was experiencing this intimacy with Him. I had been trusting Him at His Word. I had been sitting with Him at His feet and learning how to walk through the storms of my life believing Him, trusting Him at His Word. I could no longer be satisfied by the relationship I had with Him. Now I needed everything. Now I needed more than I even knew was there for me.

When Ronnie died, I found myself at the place of trusting Jesus but not having a clue about what to do next. I had hoped in Him alone and His promises to me were that everything was going to be all right. So, now I clung to Him to find that place. The place where everything was going to be okay, though nothing was okay in the natural world.

I knew that I could not make a decision about who God was based upon my situation. I would continue trusting and pressing in. Now I had only Him, and I wasn't going to change who I knew He was and what He had become for me. I had a choice in those moments after Ronnie had passed into the fullness of life. *I had the option to be overcome by my circumstances or to be overcome by the One who held me in my circumstances.*

My heart wanted an answer. My heart wanted to know and understand so that I could make sense of it. My reasoning mind wanted an answer to put a box around everything and tie it neatly with a bow, and make my experience into a theology.

> I had the option to be overcome by my circumstances or to be overcome by the One who held me in my circumstances.

When our heart wants to find an answer, we can come to the wrong conclusions. We can begin reasoning with our mind and form an opinion of who God is based entirely on our situation rather than who He said He is. God is the same yesterday, today, and tomorrow. Our circumstances in life sway like the wind, but He never changes.

I could not change who the Word of God said He is. God did not change from the night that we prayed and believed for Ronnie's healing to the morning when I found Ronnie gone and in Heaven.

When I awoke the next morning after the beautiful time of prayer with Kate and Tom, I discovered that Ronnie wasn't next to me in bed. I quickly got up to see where he had gone. As I came around the bed, all I could do was cry out, "NO."

Ronnie lay on the floor. I could tell from his position that he had been there for hours. I ran over and fell next to him. He was gone. His body was still there with me, but he was not there anymore.

Questions ran through my mind.

How did I not wake up?

How could the Lord let him go and me not be there with him?

How could he be gone after we had such a beautiful time with the presence of Heaven in our room last night?

What am I going to do?

Is this real, or am I going to wake up from my bad dream?

They say you should pinch yourself if you think you are dreaming, so I literally pinched myself to be sure that this wasn't a dream.

I remember sitting next to Ronnie and saying to the Lord, "You told me that everything was going to be okay, but it doesn't look like that right now."

At that moment, I had a choice. I chose Jesus. I chose to look at my husband who was dead and say to Jesus, "I'm going to trust that You will show me how this is going to be okay. You said You only have good things for me; I can't see them now, but by faith, I receive them into my heart."

It was good for Ronnie. He was completely healed and living the fullness of life at the same time that our children and I were facing the reality of his absence from our daily lives. We were facing how to live out "everything is going to be okay" as we faced each day without Ronnie.

I had nothing else to hold on to, nowhere else to run for strength and peace. I only had Jesus, and I didn't want to choose anything but Him. I knew how good He had been to us. I had seen the beauty of His love for us over the past five months. Jesus was the same in the moment of Ronnie passing

110

into Heaven as He had been those past five months as He walked with us, strengthened us, gave us peace, and whispered of His healing power in Ronnie's body. This is the tension we have as believers. Jesus is good as we trust Him for healing, and He is good as Ronnie entered into His presence and into eternity. God is good. The reality that I walked into that morning was that God is good. This time did not change my decision of who I believe God is. That would make my reasoning a theology so that I could understand my circumstance. There may be times in our lives when we will only know that God is good, and everything else remains unanswered until Heaven.

As we walk intimately with Jesus, trusting Him above our thoughts or reasoning mind, above how this world functions and is moved by sin and separated from God our Father, there will be questions and circumstances that we cannot answer. This is faith. This is trust in the One who knows. I am relieved from the burden of having to know and understand. I am relieved from the pressure of having to control things so that they make sense in this natural world. I am thankful that we don't have the responsibility of holding all things together. It's Jesus' responsibility.

> There may be times in our lives when we will only know that God is good.

Colossians 1:16–17 (AMPC) states, "For it was in Him that all things were created in heaven and on earth, things seen and things unseen, whether thrones, dominions, rulers, or authorities; all things were created and exist through Him [by His service, intervention] and in and for Him. And He Himself existed before all things, and in Him all things consist (cohere, are held together)."

What do we do? We trust in His Word, in His truth, and in His ways. As we trust, we don't change the truth to make sense of our reality. We change our reality to line up with His truth. What does that mean? It means I have control over my choices and decisions. In those choices and decisions, I spend time knowing what His truth is so that I can line myself up with what He says. His promise is that only then will I live the fullness of life till it overflows, and He will always be with me, and I will never be put to shame for trusting Him. The outcome is a fullness of life spent in His presence, now and in eternity. His promise is that it's all going to be okay. Not because of the circumstances, but because of the inner life that you're living with Him in the intimacy of the Bridal Chamber.

When I think back to the moment I found Ronnie, I realize I never questioned God being good and not helping me through. Somewhere in my heart, I had grown to know that He is always good, and it's always going to be okay because of who He is. I am amazed at how walking through the months of Ronnie and me believing for complete healing this side of Heaven led me to this unwavering trust in Jesus.

"Do two walk together unless they have agreed to do so?" (Amos 3:3 NIV)

Ronnie and I had agreed to walk together with the Lord, trusting in Him and Him alone. This was the position that I continued to keep. I decided to walk with the Lord, and I wasn't going to move from the solid ground I stood on.

During the days leading up to the funeral, we were surrounded by prayers and kept in a bubble of grace. Because of my background in the funeral business with my father, I knew that Ronnie was gone and only his shell that housed his born-again spirit was left behind. It was amazing to me that even though I had cared for so many bodies of loved ones, I now fully realized this truth when looking at Ronnie. He was gone. He didn't even look the same.

With all of the activity, I kept my heart and mind busy so that I didn't wander to feeling sorry for myself or my children. We pressed on and prepared to celebrate Ronnie's life. I stayed steady at Jesus' feet, in His Word, and listening to His voice. This was what sustained me.

The morning of his funeral, January 3rd, I was reading from Proverbs 3:5–6. These verses, though very familiar to me, spoke to my heart that morning.

"Trust in *and* rely confidently on the LORD with all your heart
And do not rely on your own insight *or* understanding.
In all your ways know *and* acknowledge *and* recognize Him,
And He will make your paths straight *and* smooth [removing obstacles that block your way]."

It was the word "know" in verse 6 that became my desire that day. In the midst of honoring Ronnie, in the midst of my pain, I longed to know the Lord. In the midst of us not understanding why Ronnie had not recovered, I wanted to know Jesus' heart for me, His love for me as He carried me through a day that I had prayed I'd never have to live through.

My focus was holding onto Jesus, keeping steady, as we discovered what life was going to be like. I was discovering my position in the Bridal Chamber where fear and emotions had no place. It was Jesus we had walked with, and now it was time for me to discover Him more completely.

Journal Entries

12/31/12

"Passing through the valley of weeping, they make it a place of springs; the early rain also fills the pools with blessing" (Psalm 84:6). Hallelujah, we pass through and make it a place of springs. Lord, I commit this passing through to You and trust You to make it a place springing forth full of blessing. That's what You do.

Verse 12: "O Lord of hosts, blessed (happy, fortunate, to be envied) is the man who trusts in You [leaning and believing on You, committing all and confidently looking to You and that without fear or misgiving]."

1/2/13

I praise God for His presence and love. I know as I seek Him I will find Him, and I can wake early to be with Him. As I sat here searching for a Scripture for Ronnie's memorial folder, I was reminded of the verse that the Lord gave me as I waited for Ronnie to overcome fear and ask me to marry him. Isaiah 42:16 gave me great peace, and it does now as I embark into the unknown. "And I will bring the blind by a way that they know not; I will lead them in paths that they have not known. I will make darkness into light before them and make uneven places into a plain. These things I have determined to do for them; and I will not leave them forsaken." Thank You, Holy Spirit, for leading me and guiding me. I am blind in my flesh but have great sight in my faith!

"Behold the former things have come to pass, and new things I now declare; before they spring forth I tell you of them!" (Isaiah 42:7) Thank You, Lord! You declare them before we see them. You give us our sight. May I see and believe and trust and know that they will come to pass whether I see them or not; what You declare will come to pass! Hallelujah!!

1/19/13

Praise You, Lord, for this beautiful sunrise and a day filled full of Your mercy and grace. I am so thankful for You, Lord, and Your love. I invite You into my loss, which is too big for me to comprehend. I invite You in and thank You for Your love for me and How You fill me full to overflowing with Your comfort and grace. Thank You, Holy Spirit, for filling me full today—a fountain filling me full to overflowing. Mourning may last for a night, but joy comes in the morning. Thank You, Lord, that I am entering into a time of great joy and abundance in You. Joy springing up, joy bubbling over. Thank You, Lord. It's not dependent upon my circumstances but upon You and Your faithfulness to us. Thank You, Lord, that Ben, Daniel, and Lydia are entering into a fullness they have never known before. Hallelujah!

1/20/13

Praise You, Lord Jesus. Praise You for Your wondrous works and Your beautiful handiwork, for Your truths that never change—they will stand until the end of time. Hallelujah, You are God, and Your truths never change, Your promises are true and on You I can depend!

Psalm 6. I have cried, grieved, my pillow is full of my tears, the Lord has heard the voice of my weeping, the Lord receives my prayer and lets all my enemies be put to shame. Thank You, Lord, that You do hear my prayer, my cry in the night. You alone hear me and have mercy and compassion for me. Praise You, Lord Jesus! Lord, You are our Redeemer, Restorer, Righteous Judge, Protector. I have experienced redemption in You for all things lost in my past—even things lost from my choices. Lord Jesus, I thank You that You will redeem for my children and me everything that has been lost/stolen from our lives. I trust You for that; I trust You to do that for my children and that we will receive that which is even greater than what we perceive to have been stolen. For what You give is always far greater; it comes and overtakes us and overwhelms me! I submit myself to You, Lord; I give You my grief, my loss, my pain, and I receive all that You have for me today.

Application Questions

1. Have you prayed for something, hoped for something, and it did not come to pass?
2. In the midst of things that turned out differently than your hopes, have you made a decision about who God was in the midst of the circumstance?
3. Does this understanding of God line up with the truth of God's Word?
4. How would it have looked if you didn't allow the circumstance to define God but you allowed God to define your circumstance?
5. In your present circumstances, journal who you believe God is for you. As you read what you have written, have these understandings of who God is come out of a need to define Him or who He promises to be for you?
6. Ask the Holy Spirit to reveal to you any beliefs you have about God, Jesus, and the Holy Spirit that do not line up with His truth. Openly receive what He is showing you. Ask the Holy Spirit to help you replace this belief with the truth.

CHAPTER 10

Laying it all down

When we enter the Bridal Chamber, the coverings fall away so that we are completely uncovered in the presence of Jesus. In the intimacy of the Bridal Chamber, we know the One who loves us, and though we are vulnerable and exposed, there is peace and trust in our heart. It is safe. We are willing to take off those things that once kept us hidden. We desire to do this in His presence because of our deep and passionate love for Him, which comes from His ravished heart for us.

When I entered into that intimate Bridal Chamber and took off all of my covering, I began to realize that my emotions and pain were coverings, and I needed to lay them down to be one with Jesus.

It is possible to hold on so tightly to what we feel that those emotions keep us apart from Him. We can decide in our heart that we want to hold on to what we feel more than we want to open our heart, our hands, to what He has for us. We can become so familiar and comfortable with what we feel and know to be true that we become unaware of what

He offers. We can use those emotions as a covering to decide how we will walk through our life, our storms.

Here in the Bridal Chamber, there is no desire to hold on to those emotions in the midst of His love. This intimacy we have with Him fills our heart with everything that we desire so that we know it is safe to lay those feelings down and receive what He has for us in that moment of pain, grief, anger, hurt, betrayal, etc.

We are human. We are a body, a soul, and a spirit. We do feel. Jesus has great compassion for our feelings and emotions. He exhibited emotion while he walked this earth as a man.

So many people showed their love and concern for my family and me. The kindness and outpouring were overwhelming. The generosity of families bringing meals to us for almost three months helped me more than anyone could imagine because I could take care of the kids and myself and maintain a life of normalcy without having to think about fixing dinner. It was probably all of those little things that made such a huge difference for our family.

The words that people shared about who Ronnie had been to them were words that I cherish in my heart. Cards were sent to me for months from people wanting to tell me how they were keeping us in their prayers and how they were so sorry for our loss.

People were sorry for our loss.

I'm not sure what happened in my heart, but as those words were spoken or written to me almost daily, they became a weight on my soul. The whisper I heard in my heart was that people felt sorry for me and that my children and I had less than others had, that somehow we would trudge on with only part of what we needed. The rest of what we needed was gone. These words attempted to grip me and take me down. The words were well intended, but they carried a weight that was trying to take me out.

A few weeks after Ronnie's funeral, I was talking to the Lord about how those words were weighing on me and making me feel like we had less than what others had because Ronnie was now with Him. I had decided in my heart, after Ronnie's death, that we were going to live the overcoming life that Jesus died to give to us, and my children would live as great a life as they always had even though their father was gone. I did not want anything to happen to their dreams or their day-to-day life that would cause them to stumble and fall.

The Lord whispered to my heart, "There is no loss in Me, there is only gain. Ronnie has gained the fullness of life here with Me, and you and your children will live the fullness of life in Me."

Scripture says, "For to live is Christ and to die is gain" (Philippians 1:21).

I can tell you that I did not feel the truth of what Jesus was saying to me. I knew His Words were true and that they were life to me. So every time someone would tell me they were sorry for my loss or the enemy would whisper about all the things that I had lost, I would declare, "There is no loss in Jesus, only gain, and Ronnie, our children, and I are living the fullness of life in Jesus."

At first, nothing changed in my heart when I started declaring this. But it wasn't long before my outlook, my thoughts, and my days aligned with that truth. Jesus knew what I needed to hear, and as I remained with Him in that intimate place, the Bridal Chamber, and took my fears, my brokenness, my pain to Him, He always gave me everything I needed.

The Words that Jesus spoke to my heart framed my experience. How we choose to look at a situation is how that situation will be framed in our soul. As we move forward, that framing will decide if we look at it from God's perspective or the world's perspective. Our framing will decide if it will be a stronghold in our mind that keeps us from moving forward, or if it will be a place of freedom and an experience of who Jesus is. Every time that we look back or remember it, it can either bring peace and hope, or fear, pain, and dread.

I didn't understand how it was possible, but joy actually began erupting from my spirit and bubbling over into my soul. How could that possibly happen in such a short time after my husband went to be with Jesus? I don't know. I only know that by declaring how Jesus saw my circumstance, He took my grief and loss and gave me life. I was choosing not to hold on to the emotions, but to live the fullness that Jesus said was mine. It was mine even in the darkest of my circumstances because His fullness of life is not dependent upon circumstances. It is dependent upon me agreeing with who He is and what He has already given us.

I didn't step outside of that protective, intimate place with Him. I stayed very near to Him, receiving everything that I needed for myself and my children. I took my questions and my thoughts to Him, and He gave me a truth to live on for each day.

By laying my emotions or my feelings down, I allowed Jesus to minister to the deepest places in my heart. He was also showing me what His truth was for me in that place of hurt. I was able to find Him and His truth because I wasn't holding onto the dreadful feeling of losing my husband.

I had every opportunity to look at my situation as a complete disappointment and abandonment from God. After all, we trusted Him completely and never stopped believing that Ronnie would be healed. I could let this experience, not the Word, define who Jesus was.

Wanting answers for the situations in our lives can open us up to a doctrine that is part truth and part lie. It can lead us to define Jesus through the eyes of our circumstances rather than the truth of His Word. We can only receive what we believe to be true. His Word and His whispers of love and truth to my heart were what I needed to remain on the path to healing and victory.

My emotions came out of the hurt in my heart, out of the emptiness because Ronnie was gone. My emotions are not truth. I have shared that many times in this book. Emotions come out of our soul, out of our experiences and the beliefs that we carry from those circumstances. To live from our spirit man where the fullness of life—the *dunamis* power of Christ—resides, we have to let go of those thoughts and emotions. As we lay those down and choose to live out of what is deep inside us, it begins to be released until it floods into our soul.

As I declared those words of gain and took them as my truth. Everything else I felt had to bow to that.

We feel what we feel.

We need to allow our feelings out and experience what they are so that we don't stuff them down and cause further pain and suffering down the road.

It isn't good to ignore what you are feeling.

If that is what you are feeling, then that's okay—just go with it because there is nothing you can do to change it.

It's okay to feel that way because you should feel that way walking through this experience.

These are all phrases that we have heard before about our feelings.

If each person feels something different while going through the same experience, then which feeling is the truth? What each of us feels is a true emotion, but the question is, if it comes from our soul, does that mean it is the truth in that situation?

"To the Jews who had believed him, Jesus said, 'If you hold to my teaching, you are really my disciples. Then you will know the truth, and the truth will set you free'" (NIV, John 8:31–32).

"Jesus answered, 'I am the way and the truth and the life. No one comes to the Father except through me'" (NIV, John 14:6).

The only truth is Jesus. He is perfect truth. He does not change with the shifting of shadows. He is the same yesterday, today, and tomorrow.

I came to realize—as I walked through Ronnie's death and sought after the Lord for strength to endure each day—that I could give Him my emotions and then experience His truth. Each day after Ronnie's death, there was a crevice, a chasm of pain that wanted to swallow me up and take me down. I didn't want to walk through my days clawing along the ground, hoping to stay out of the pit.

I'll never forget the pain I had one day soon after Ronnie's death. I was coming home from running errands. The kids were at school, and a worship song came on the radio. It was the song "Yours Will Be the Only Name" by Big Daddy Weave. As I sang along, I was driving into my garage. When I closed the garage door, I felt such emptiness and ache in my heart that I cried out, but there was no sound. No words came from my lips, only moans from the pain. I knew I couldn't sit in my car anymore, so I got up and dragged myself into the house. I wasn't crawling, but it took all I had to put one foot in front of the other. The groceries would have to wait—I had no energy to bring anything with me. I stumbled through the kitchen, into the family room, and fell into a chair. The dogs, who were always excited to see me, just stared with their heads cocked, not understanding what was wrong with me. The sun shone in through the windows, and I just crumbled into the chair like a rag doll. I felt so broken and empty inside with no strength to hold myself up. I cried out to the Lord for His healing love to come like a balm to fill the empty cavern in my heart. There was absolutely nothing in this world that I could stuff down into that place to fill it. Nothing would have filled that hole. It was like the Grand Canyon waiting to swallow me up.

As I sat there crying and receiving His love, the pain began to ease. I was able to let go of it. I didn't want it; it would not help me or take me anywhere but down. As I continued to sit and receive His love, the pain became less and less. I was able to sit up within a few minutes, wiping away the tears that had washed my makeup down my face, neck, and clothing. I could breathe again. I could take deep breaths and stay calm, no longer cry uncontrollably.

I discovered that though my pain was too much for me, Jesus was more than enough to carry it away. Whenever the pain came, I went to Jesus and received His love. The number of times I went to Him in uncontrollable tears became fewer and fewer. Soon, I got to the point that whenever I began feeling that pain and emptiness, I would go to Him before the tears could even start, and He would take it away.

As I went to Jesus for His healing, He showed me that I didn't have to hold the pain. I would invite Him in, and He would give me peace. He would fill my emptiness. I had joy instead of mourning. Joy was mine because of all He was doing for me. His healing power made me alive, and I was so thankful for all He had done for me. My focus was on all that He was rather than all that I no longer had.

People told me that it would be hard for months after Ronnie was gone, that it was okay to grieve for as long as I needed. This was normal. People expected me to experience that pain and misery. To me, it was a miracle of God's love that I did not walk through a long period of grief. God's love healed my heart so that I didn't have to feel pain from Ronnie's loss. I didn't need to look for things to fill my emptiness.

They would never be able to accomplish what God did for me anyway.

I had known pain and loss in my life. I know how grieving can keep me in a very empty place, and I have no desire to stay there. I knew that I could not be there for my children and continue moving forward with my life if I camped in that place. The Lord had told me that Ronnie was living the fullness of life and that there was no loss for any of us in Him as we walked through this valley. I chose to believe Him and receive all that He had for me in the midst of my experience.

The Lord gave me and others visions of Ronnie in that fullness of life. When Ronnie was first admitted to the hospital, before we knew what was wrong in his body, he would wake up throughout the night. Being all alone in the hospital room, he would talk with the Lord. One night, he told me he was talking to the Lord about all He had done. Ronnie had asked the Lord that night to show him all of His many wonders. Ronnie tried to tell me what the Lord had shown him, but he would get so overcome with emotion from what he had seen that he was never able to share it all with me. He was able to tell me that the Lord was showing him the beauty of the covenant of the Lord with His Bride. I had never shared this with anyone, so it was only Ronnie and me who knew what he had asked that night in the hospital room.

A few days after Ronnie died, the kids and I went to Sunday morning church services. Kate saved us a few seats in front of her and her family who was visiting from California. It was such a comfort to see them there. I wasn't sure how I would get through being at church without Ronnie. After the service, I hugged Kate's daughter-in-law, Amanda, and welcomed her to Iowa. Amanda has such a sweet spirit and sensitivity to the Lord, and I have always loved her heart. As we were talking, she asked if she could share something she saw by the Spirit during worship. It was about Ronnie, but she wanted to be sure that I was okay hearing it. I immediately said yes, because I wanted to hear everything that the Lord wanted to reveal to us.

Amanda shared that she had seen Ronnie sitting underneath a tree. He was younger and wasn't wearing glasses, dressed in comfortable clothing: jeans and a plaid shirt. He was sitting reading a book titled, *The Many Wonders of God*. She wanted to share how he looked healthy and at peace reading a book under the tree.

I could only smile and give her a hug. She had no idea that that was the question Ronnie had asked of the Lord, and now he was in Heaven a few days after he arrived, relaxing and reading a book on the subject. He was receiving the answer to his question. This picture made me so happy.

There were many times when I was missing Ronnie, the emptiness trying to drag me in, and I would think about Ronnie and the life he was now living. This picture brought me peace. How could I be sad for myself that he was gone when I knew that he was living the fullness of life in Heaven and learning about the very thing he wondered about here on earth?

The Lord continually took care of my every need. After Ronnie's death, it was hard for me when I felt my wedding ring on my finger. Rather than bringing me peace, it was a constant reminder that he was no longer with me. Though I may not have talked with the Lord directly about this, He knew my heart. One Sunday in worship, as I closed my eyes and focused on Him, I saw with my spiritual eyes a beautiful ring that had vines intertwined between two thin rows of diamonds. It was larger than life and beautiful. In my heart, I asked the Lord, "What is this?" He whispered, "I am the vine and you are in Me now." I remember telling Him how beautiful it was and how His Words ministered to my heart.

I went home that day to see if the ring even existed or if I would have to design it. Amazingly, as I searched the internet I found that exact ring. I was overwhelmed with His love for me. I enlisted my friend to come with me to go look at it in the mall the next week.

As I looked at the ring and shared my story with the salesperson, I felt peace about moving forward with the purchase, so I went ahead and ordered it in my size. As we left the store and went through another store to get to our cars, I walked by a display of t-shirts and was caught by surprise. There, hanging on the end of the rack, was a t-shirt that said, "Love you, me." That was how Ronnie and I always signed our quick e-mails to one another throughout the day. All I could do was stand there and cry. I knew that the Lord was confirming to my heart that it was okay for me to begin wearing this new ring.

Over the following months as I wore this ring, I would look down, see it on my finger, and receive peace that I was in Jesus now. I wasn't alone. I was found in Him, I lived in Him, and everything I needed was from Him. My heart would be continually settled by His love for me.

As time continues to move forward, I have meditated on what the Lord showed me as He ministered His love to my heart, took my pain, and gave me peace and even joy in Him. Through the experience of choosing His heart and truth for me in the midst of my heartache from Ronnie's leaving, I am learning to invite His truth into everyday life.

The experience of being in the intimacy of the Bridegroom's love for me keeps me from being dragged around by my emotions through the ups and downs of this world. Two verses give me such hope for receiving a greater understanding in this area for my life.

"I will not speak with you much longer, for the ruler of the world (Satan) is coming. And he has no claim on Me [no

power over Me nor anything that he can use against Me]..."
(John 14:30).

"...[looking away from all that will distract us and] focusing our eyes on Jesus, who is the Author and Perfecter of faith [the first incentive for our belief and the One who brings our faith to maturity], who for the joy [of accomplishing the goal] set before Him endured the cross, disregarding the shame, and sat down at the right hand of the throne of God [revealing His deity, His authority, and the completion of His work]" (Hebrews 12:2).

The enemy had no claim, nothing in common, with Jesus. His soul was completely free from the enemy. And when Jesus went to the cross, He went with joy in His heart because He knew what it would accomplish. He had a choice about what He would experience. He chose joy because His eyes weren't on Himself and the pain He was going to endure. His eyes were on you and what you would receive as He took all of your sins, shame, guilt, pain, sorrow, poverty, sickness, and disease.

It is because of all that Jesus accomplished on the cross that each one of us can release our emotions to Him. It can be scary to let go of what we are feeling. As we live in the intimacy of the Bridal Chamber, we learn to let go and accept what He has to give us. We learn not to allow the enemy access into our lives through our emotions and painful circumstances. We can receive His truth and let go of everything else.

Let go and take hold of all that He has for you.

Journal Entries

1/23/13

Lord Jesus, we need You; we need You so much. The hole in our lives is huge, and there is nothing that can fill it except

You. I ask that by Your Spirit today, Ben, Daniel, Lydia, and I will receive the depth, the width, and the breadth of YOUR LOVE, MERCY, AND GRACE FOR US.

Lord, Your Word says that You are my husband and the children's Father. I don't know how to help each one of them connect with You in that way. Only You know, Father, how to reach them and show them that, so I thank You that by Your Spirit it happens. Thank You, Holy Spirit and ministering angels of Heaven that come and minister to my children's hearts.

"Since by your obedience to the truth through the Holy Spirit you have purified your hearts for the sincere affection of the brethren" (1 Peter 1:22). My obedience to the truth, standing on the truth, performs a work in me. Not only does my faith please the Lord God Almighty, but it cleanses me, breaks off the lies and bad fruit, and helps me to love others. Thank You, Lord; that has been my prayer for so long, that You would change me, transform me so that I can love others above and before myself, and love You more than anything in my life! Lydia, Daniel, Ben, and I do not live a life out of loss, but of deep fulfillment, a life that is overflowing even in the presence of great loss! That fullness is the power of the Holy Spirit within us! The truth of Jesus in us. Glory to God!

Deuteronomy 28. My world got ripped apart, but my sure foundation is Jesus Christ – on Christ the solid Rock I stand!

1/25/13

Good morning, my Lord. I'm so glad to be awake and able to come into Your presence to worship and praise You. You are my Lord; You are my everything. I worship You and bless You this morning, Lord. Hallelujah, it's a brand new day in the kingdom of God. Bless the Lord, oh my soul, and all that is within me, bless His holy name. Bless the Lord, oh my soul, and forget not all of His benefits, who heals all of my diseases, forgives me all my iniquities and restores my life from the pit.

1/28/13

Thank You, Holy Spirit, that You guide me through this new land, helping me to endure and stay steady, even being full of joy in this new land as You help me to keep my eyes on Jesus so I will have grace, which empowers me to endure the journey! As I begin to understand how You delight in me as Your bride, Lord, I will be established in a place of increasing strength and equipped to face the coming days. Lord, may my life be a picture, a reflection, of Your love for Your bride and how I am enabled, equipped, and empowered in my true identity to live for You in ways I have never known before.

2/11/13

Praise You Lord Jesus I am Yours and You are mine! That's everything, it doesn't get any better than that! You are my love, my one desire. This earth has nothing for me compared to the gift of You, the fullness and truth of You Lord. I agree with Heaven today! I agree with the truth of Heaven over my life today. I have nothing missing and nothing broken. I am redeemed, restored, righteous and deeply blessed of the Lord. Hallelujah. It is a great day today because of all You are in me and over me! May Daniel and Lydia receive that hope in their hearts as they rest so when they awake they may look at their day with hope and expectation. May Ben be filled full of Your hope and expectation Lord, may he mature into the man You have called him to be, so that he is prepared and ready for all You have planned and purposed for him.

I love you Lord. I come to You to hear Your voice and to be changed by You, to receive one Word or one touch from

You because it will change me forever. I praise You Lord, thank you Lord. You are my hope and firm foundation. In You I hope and trust, in You and You alone Lord, in You and You alone. Praise You Jesus Hallelujah. Lord Jesus abundance, abundant hope, abundant help in time of need. You are my hope abundantly, You are my abundance, my hope eternal. Wind blowing outside. May Your Spirit blow across this land, blow away the dross, blow away that which entangles that we might humbly seek You Lord, humbly come into Your presence and worship You and adore You and You alone.

Went to go look at the ring I had seen in the Spirit, the vine diamond ring. The Lord is my Bridegroom, He is the vine and I am the branch. He is my source. The ring was beautiful. As I went back through the store there was a shirt and it said: "love you, me." I had just been talking about the ring and Ronnie. It caught me off guard, but felt it was a confirmation that I was to buy the ring. God is my supply.

Application Questions

1. What are you holding onto that keeps you away from intimacy with Christ?
2. Do you believe in your heart that your identity is being one with Christ as His Bride?
3. Are there places in your heart where you have a hard time believing that He is good and has only good things for you?
4. Which is bigger—your desire for Him or your desire for other things?
5. How does not knowing everything in your walk with Jesus affect your daily trust in Him?

CHAPTER 11

No Turning Back

Changes. New seasons. We all experience these in our life. Some come from decisions we make, some are due to the age and stage we enter, and some come from circumstances totally out of our control. No matter what causes these transformations, we will have to adjust to the new that comes along with them.

Have you ever noticed that when we enter into new things, we compare them to the way things used to be? Our brains are so used to the paths we've been walking down every day that when we have a change, whether big or small, we compare it.

We can complain about it, but resistance to the inevitable only keeps us from moving forward. It can keep us from finding the blessing and the good things in our new situation. The past can become a ball and chain that we drag around and bring out every time we have to do something different.

This is where I found myself after Ronnie died. There were so many things that he took care of even though he was traveling most weekdays. I remember being at the hardware store having to buy light bulbs for the can lights and different lamps around the house. He always took care of this. So when there were no bulbs to replace the burned out ones, I found myself in the light bulb aisle.

If you are thinking what a little thing this was to deal with, you are probably right. The real issue was that it reminded me of how Ronnie was gone, and I now had to take care of everything. I had no clue what bulbs to buy, so after my first trip down the light bulb aisle with no success, I went home.

For my second attempt, I took the burned out bulbs with me. Do you have any idea how many options there are for can lights? I remember standing there and wanting to cry. All I could think was, "He's gone, and now I have to figure this out. Why did he have to go? I don't want to have to do this. I want Ronnie back."

I am so glad that no one paid any attention to me because I stood staring at boxes while tears rolled down my cheeks. It was incredibly lonely standing there. People walked by, but I was so alone. I couldn't leave without my light bulbs because I had done that the day before. The kitchen was getting dark at night.

"Jesus, I need You."

Taking a deep breath, I took the bulbs out of the bag and began looking for replacements. The Holy Spirit was going to have to help me with this one. All I wanted to do was get the bulbs and get out of there.

Thankfully, it wasn't long before I was checked out with what I hoped were replacements for our lights.

These new tasks happened over and over again.

Ronnie died right after Christmas. We had put the garland up a few weeks before Christmas, and since it wasn't artificial, it started looking pretty bad by February. On a rare nice day in February, I took the ladder out to the front porch to take it all down.

If I hadn't helped him put it up, I would have had no idea how to cut it down. This was another thing he did for all of us. The artificial stems that I put in the pots were stored in the garage. I was able to pull those out. The containers we stored them in were on shelves above the garage doors. I stood in the garage and wondered how I was going to get those containers down while standing on a ladder.

I cried out to the Lord again about how much I didn't want to do this. How was I going to, and why—why is this the way it had to go, with me here and Ronnie with Him?

I don't know how I managed to do all of it that day. I only know that the Lord gave me the strength to keep pressing on, taking care of the things that needed to be done. They were done through a lot of tears and a flood of memories of Ronnie doing all of this for us.

When I had to begin mowing our big backyard, I decided to tackle this in a completely different way. Dwelling on the memories was not making any of it easier. So this time, I decided that I would sing praises while I was mowing. I knew I had to take my eyes off the old and press on into the new, and the only way I was going to be able to do that was by putting my eyes on Jesus.

I got my iPod and my earphones and cranked it up. Thank goodness the mower was loud because I sang at the top of my lungs. He lifted my eyes through praise and took my focus off what I was doing. As my attention turned to Him, He began speaking to my heart about how much He loved me and how He was there for me. He told me about how blessed I was to have had Ronnie do all these things for me. Jesus was with me now. He was going to help me move forward. I remember Jesus telling me that I couldn't bring the way it used to be into the way it is now. I needed to look at what was behind me, count it all blessed, and close the door. My future did not include the past dragging behind me. My future was in Him, and the comparison of the past couldn't come along.

God is so wise. He wanted me to focus on the blessing that my life had been, rather than comparing it to my current life. The freedom that I felt in focusing on all the blessings and closing the door was empowering. It didn't mean I was forgetting. It meant that I didn't have to drag Ronnie around with me in my new life and feel the emptiness of his absence through everything that I now had to do. It allowed me to keep him in my heart as a blessing, an amazing gift, and then find the blessings in each and every new day.

I could trust the Lord and what He told me because He was there for me each and every step of the way. I could trust that He wasn't making me forget Ronnie, but that He was helping me to move into all that He had for me. If I chose to continue comparing my new life to the life I had, I would miss out on receiving all that He had for me. I would remain stuck and focused on the loss.

The Lord's plans for our children and me didn't end when Ronnie died. His plans for us continued. His Word says that they are good plans, plans for a future and a hope.

"'For I know the plans *and* thoughts that I have for you,' says the LORD, 'plans for peace *and* well-being and not for disaster to give you a future and a hope'" (Jeremiah 29:11).

Today, as I am writing this chapter, my middle child, Daniel, is attending his last day of high school. How appropriate for me to write these words to you while experiencing the closing of a door and an entrance to the future. As I looked at the pictures of his first day of kindergarten and the photo I took of him on the front porch before he left for school, my heart missed those wonderful days when he was our little guy in elementary school. My thoughts went to the wonderful memories as well as the things that I wish we had done and the things that have been taken away.

Today, as Daniel experiences his last day of high school, I get to experience Jesus as my Redeemer. My Redeemer for everything that my heart aches for: the experiences that I feel empty from not experiencing. Jesus is my Redeemer, and He can fill my heart to overflowing. As His Bride, I can give my thoughts to Him and receive an overflowing heart full of His love in return. I am so overwhelmed by His love for me that it is impossible for me to feel that anything has ever been missing or stolen.

To walk through the door into all the new that has been given to us, we need to close the door to what has been and receive all Jesus has for us. Receive His truths and receive His redeeming love. Whether the experiences from the past left us wanting more or if they were full, either way—in faith, we can close the door and enter into all the new that He has for us.

Journal Entries

2/16/13

Praise You, Lord. My desire is to come and be with You early, as I first awake, that I may come into Your presence and minister to You with praise, thanksgiving, and sweet communion with You, Lord. Lord, You are my desire, You are my one desire, there is nothing that I would want besides You, Lord. I'm an eternal being because I was born again in Christ Jesus. Though I live in a mortal body, my spirit within me is now greater than the limitations of my soul and body. As I live in the depth of this new life—eternal life—my mind, will, emotions, desires, and body must come into subjection to the Spirit of God within me so that more and more glory and light are released…to set people free…to release His love so that they too may get lost in the depths of His love.

I hear the Lord's voice whispering, "It's all going to be okay. The depths of my love will consume you; it consumes all of your pain and loss and washes it away. There is never loss in Me, My child. I have you; I've got this for you. I have all of your life in my hands. Yes, you look back at your life from this time and see lots of messiness, brokenness, and mess-ups. I look back at your life and see My beautiful daughter getting set free and healed, walking in trust, allowing the Word to wrap around her and work within her. You look forward from this point in time, and you see a vast unknown. I see my redeemed daughter, My Bride, restored with nothing missing, walking in love, setting the captives free, releasing them from their prisons and healing their broken hearts. I see a woman standing on a solid rock, invincible to the enemy, wrapped in raiment of clothing that shines in glory, enraptured by the love of her Savior and never alone, full of joy and laughter, never confused, humble before her God, and walking and running in total freedom. I see her, girl, and that's you. I've got this, it's all going to be okay, and I will never leave you or forsake you. Everything you need, I've got for you. See the cross as the key. See the treasure that is poured out, the treasure of everything you need being wide open on the other side of the cross. See the cross, but always see what it accomplished, what it opened for you. My blood is a river, a fountain; you are washed, My daughter. You are washed, and everything comes clean in the river, and it flows; it makes glad. There is nothing I would withhold from you, My darling. I promise you that you will have everything you need and ask for. As you see it, you will receive it."

2/22/13

Lord, I am so thankful that You are bigger, abounding in goodness, power, and love over my hurts, pains, and troubles.

You are so amazing, and I come to You this morning to find You, to praise You, to minister to Your heart with songs of praise and thanksgiving. I need You more, more than I ever needed You before; I need You. Holy Spirit, I invite You here in my time; teach me not only now but all day long that all day I may be in Your presence and feel the intimacy of the presence all day long, and be about my Father's business all day long. I know Jesus loves me because He died for me; may I become more intimately aware of His love for me.

"The secret of the sweet satisfying companionship of the Lord have they who fear (revere and worship) Him, and He will show them His covenant and reveal to them its [deep, inner] meaning" (Psalm 25:14). Hallelujah, sounds like a promise to me.

Psalm 27:4–6, 8, 13–14. Praise You, Jesus. I thank You for the intimacy of Your presence. You satisfy me in the secret place; peace, joy, and strength fill me in the secret place.

5/4/13

Last night, a wonderful 180 zone banquet.... But sad to be there alone and sad to be there with other couples...and very sad because my Ronnie would have loved it and cried with every testimony. I miss him, Jesus. I really don't want to be doing life without him. I have no desire to be alone or living my life this way. I will press on and live in You, and receive the depth of Your love to live out my life, fulfill my destiny with great joy, peace, and strength. I don't want to get caught up in the natural part of my life not being what I wanted. I was created to live a supernatural life, living out of Your kingdom and the Spirit within me. The more my natural doesn't pan out, the more I delve into the spiritual kingdom where I have everything—I have righteousness, peace, and joy. I am strong. I am loved and have Your love flowing through me to others.

Lord, You are the One who satisfies my soul. You are the one who strengthens me to accomplish everything I need to in the natural realm and for Your kingdom. I need You more, Lord. I am not satisfied with the depth that I know You now. May Your Spirit take me to a deeper place in You, a deeper knowing and experiencing of Your love. Satisfy my soul, Lord; satisfy every need I have with Your love.

8/17/13

Lord Jesus, as I walk through another layer of mourning, I know that You are the only one who can satisfy the emptiness I have inside, the place in my heart that aches with longing for Ronnie.

"Make me to hear joy and gladness and be satisfied; let the bones which You have broken rejoice" (Psalm 51:8). Lord, You are the only One who satisfies me and can turn my loss into great gain. I declare in Jesus' name that my children and I do not live in loss—in You, we have great gain, joy, gladness, and are completely satisfied. May I not seek my completion in the things I do, but only in the One who completes me. Then and only then will I fulfill the desires of my heart and walk in the destiny You have for me. That I may know in my heart that You desire to fulfill me, fulfill my purpose, and raise me up in my identity in You. May I not seek those things, but seek the One who is able and worthy of all my praise and honor and thanksgiving.

2 Samuel 7:18–19. The need to take the promises of God, bring them before the Lord, and sit before Him until our perception of His beauty and power is great enough to believe that He will bring about those promises for His own glory! It is in this barren land where I come, Lord, and receive Your living water; I am able to see Your consuming fire and desire

nothing but You. For You are all I desire; You are everything that completes me and fills me.

I have taken so many blessings that You have given me and made them my comfort, my security, my identity, my strength. But here in this land where I find myself, I see that they didn't provide me any of the things I long for. Would I ask to be here? Did You want to break me by bringing me here? No, I don't even believe that You would cause circumstances in my life to bring me here. I live in a fallen world, and when I find myself in this barren place, You take it and turn it around for my good. You cause this to become a rich, fertile land full of rejoicing instead of tears, full of life instead of loss.

You are the Lover of my soul and You desire for my soul to be healed, delivered, and redeemed so that I may find my true identity and purpose in You so that my destiny is fulfilled and You receive glory upon glory, praise upon praise for who You are. May thanksgiving overflow from my heart; may I see You in all I do today, experience the depth of Your love today as I love others, pour myself out so that I am completely filled by You, my Lord.

8/26/13

All day long yesterday, as waves of grief would come I'd hear You say, "Don't look at what is behind you, look forward, keep your eyes on Me. Don't look at what you don't have, keep your eyes on Me and count it all blessed."

8/29/13

Through the night I heard the whisper in my heart, "Enter in." Lord, I enter into all You have for me. I close the door behind me, I agree with You as You close the door behind me, and step forward into all the new You have for me. May my perspective change so that as I enter in I don't bring mindsets with me, old ways of thinking.

Romans 8:5; Galatians 5:5, 16. Thank you, Lord, for your truth! I have set my mind and heart on Your truth that there is no loss in Christ, only great gain. As I have walked these eight months without Ronnie, You have given me peace, joy, and victory now at this time. As I walk forward into this new season, into all the new You have for me, I keep my heart steady in You on the truth of Your Word, which is spirit and life, and no matter the circumstances I will experience Your victory, peace, joy, and great abundant blessings. My flesh looks to the circumstances and the situation, and is moved by that, but I gratify the desires of the Holy Spirit, the Spirit in me, and live in freedom, victory, fullness of life, and peace now and forever. I am not moved by anything but Your Spirit in Jesus' name.

Application Questions

1. What situations have you walked through in the past that you continue to drag into your daily life and keep you from moving forward?
2. How can you place a different framework around the past so that as you move forward it is a positive influence on your future?
3. Are there things that have happened in the past that you need to settle so that you can move forward?
4. How are the things from the past preventing you from walking in victory in your present circumstances?
5. How can you change your perspective so that victory is yours today?

CONCLUSION

As you apply these truths to your life, I know that you will continue to have a deeper revelation of Jesus and all that He has for you. We have all of our days here on earth plus eternity to discover all of who He is. We should never attain revelation and then sit on it, expecting that knowledge or experience to be enough for our days ahead. We must always press on for more. If we are not moving forward in our relationship with Jesus, then we are not just standing still: we are moving backward. One of the beautiful things about Jesus (and they are infinite in number) is that there is always more to discover.

I heard someone say that we need to surround ourselves with other believers who are stronger than us and have a greater experience of Jesus so that we do not get comfortable and content in our relationship with Jesus. Surrounding ourselves with others who are further along in their relationship creates an awakening within us to go for more. There is a stirring in our spirit that tells us that there is more, and we hunger to attain it.

I am praying for you, my friend.

"For this reason we also, from the day we heard of it, have not ceased to pray and make [special] request for you, [asking] that you may be filled with the full (deep and clear) knowledge of His will in all spiritual wisdom [in comprehensive insight into the ways and purposes of God] and in understanding *and* discernment of spiritual things—"

"That you may walk (live and conduct yourselves) in a manner worthy of the Lord, fully pleasing to Him *and* desiring to please Him in all things, bearing fruit in every good work and steadily growing *and* increasing in *and* by the knowledge of God [with fuller, deeper, and clearer insight, acquaintance, and recognition]."

"[We pray] that you may be invigorated *and* strengthened with all power according to the might of His glory, [to exercise] every kind of endurance and patience (perseverance and forbearance) with joy,"

"Giving thanks to the Father, Who has qualified *and* made us fit to share the portion which is the inheritance of the saints (God's holy people) in the Light" (Colossians 1:9–12).

APPENDIX A

Accepting Christ as Your Lord and Savior

The Father loved us so deeply that He sent His only Son as a sacrifice in our place. Jesus did not come to condemn us, but to save us (John 3:16).

"...since all have sinned and *continually* fall short of the glory of God" (Romans 3:23).

"Because if you acknowledge *and* confess with your mouth that Jesus is Lord [recognizing His power, authority, and majesty as God], and believe in your heart that God raised Him from the dead, you will be saved" (Romans 10:9).

"He made Christ who knew no sin to [judicially] be sin on our behalf, so that in Him we would become the righteousness of God [that is, we would be made acceptable to Him and placed in a right relationship with Him by His gracious loving kindness]" (2 Corinthians 5:21).

The Word of God shows us that we fall short due to sin, and we need Jesus to save us and make our relationship right with the Father.

If you believe in your heart that Jesus is Lord, desire forgiveness for your sins, and want to be put into a right relationship with the Father, pray this prayer:

"Father, I confess that I have sinned and fall short of your glory. I believe that Jesus died on the cross in my place so that I might receive forgiveness of my sins. I receive that forgiveness now. I believe in my heart and confess with my mouth that Jesus is Lord. I invite Him into my heart to be Lord of my life. Thank you for accepting me. Thank you for washing me clean of all my sin. Thank you that I now stand in a new life in Jesus and have become His righteousness. In Jesus' name, Amen."

If you prayed this prayer, let someone close to you know. Accountability and discipleship are key to moving forward in our relationship with Jesus. I would love to pray with you and support you on this journey. Connect with me at www. ElleUnlimited.com.

APPENDIX B

Timeline

November, 1981	Abortion
November, 1987	Son Ben Was Born
April, 1997	Son Daniel Was Born
September, 1999	Miscarriage
January, 2001	Second Miscarriage
January, 2002	Healing from Abortion
January, 2003	Daughter Lydia Was Born
November, 2006	Spirit of Shame Removed
February, 2007	Experience of Jesus' Love
July, 2012	Ronnie's Diagnosis
December 28, 2012	Ronnie Walked into Eternal Life

ACKNOWLEDGEMENTS

Without the support of so many people, I would not have been able even to think that this book was possible, let alone write it. You are holding it in your hands, so I know that *all* things are possible in Christ Jesus.

The Lord has blessed me with a wonderful, loving husband after the passing of Ronnie. I never knew it would be possible to love another so deeply. God is so good. He knew the desires of my heart and blessed me with a husband who, as he says, "is my biggest fan." Without his support and belief in me and this book, I would have walked away from it many times. Thank you, Ron, for your encouragement and faith in me and my heart's passion and message. (Notice my husband's name? Jesus does have a sense of humor.)

I am so thankful for my children who stepped up and took responsibility for themselves so that I could finish this book that was burning deep within me. Thank you, Ben, Daniel, and Lydia for allowing me to go after my dream. I pray that you are released into all of the dreams that God has placed in your hearts, and you live a fulfilled, satisfied, glorified life for Jesus.

Thank you, Mom and Dad, for providing a safe and nurturing place for me to grow up. You provided a home for me to discover Jesus. All the times I walked away, you were always there to show me unconditional love so that I could put my feet back on the path the Lord has for me. Your love for me helped me understand the power of Jesus' grace and love in my life.

There have been so many women, filled with the passion of Christ, who have come alongside me throughout the years. You cried with me, prayed with me, challenged me and inspired me with your love of Christ. Thank you. Each one of you has played an integral part of this book.

NOTES

Section 1

1 Souza, Katie. *Soul Decrees*. ElevenEleven Enterprises, 2015, page xiv. ISBN 13:978-0-9883152-8-0
2 Souza, Katie. *Soul Decrees*. ElevenEleven Enterprises, 2015, page xiii. ISBN 13:978-0-9883152-8-0

Chapter 5

1 Goll, James. *Finding Hope*, BroadStreet Publishing Group, Racine, Wisconsin, USA, 2015, page 43. copyright@2015 James W. Goll ISBN 13:978-1-4245-5099-9

Chapter 7

1 Heiligenthal, Kalley, Wilson, Gabriel, Greely, Chris, Strand, Bobby. "Ever Be." Bethel Music Publishing (ASCAP), 2014. All Rights Reserved. Used by Permission
2 Thomas, Brenda. *Making the Most of Your Meltdowns*. Rhema Bible Church aka Kenneth Hagin Ministries, Inc., 2010. All rights reserved. ISBN-13:978-1-60616-876-9

Section III

1 Showers, Dr. Renald. "Jewish Marriage Customs." http://www.biblestudymanuals.net/jewish_marriage_customs.htm. Accessed May 10, 2016.

149

ABOUT THE AUTHOR

Elle Stahlhut Roetzel is an author, life coach and speaker. She has been involved with leading Bible Studies and mentoring women for over 25 years.

Her experience of Jesus in the Word has been her hope and foundation as she has walked through the many storms of her life. She firmly believes that as we begin to know whose we are, the storms that come our way will no longer move us out of peace. Instead, these experiences will be used to move us to a more intimate relationship and experience of Jesus.

Her style is authentic and aimed at the heart because she brings truth to inspire others to apply the Word in their daily lives.

She has received a Practical Ministry Certification through the International School of Ministry, is a Certified Coach through Life Forming and a Robbins-Madanes Certification Student. Her testimony of healing has been aired throughout the world on the Angel Network Channel.

In her spare time Elle enjoys swimming and boating at the lakes, biking, and spending time with her family and friends. She lives with her husband and children in Minneapolis.

You can connect with Elle at www.ElleUnlimited.com for more information about her coaching, transformational studies, speaking availability, and children's books.

The Bridal Journey

The purpose is simple
To Break Free From the Past
and the
Mindsets that Keep You From Believing the Truth
And
Begin Living Out of the Intimacy of the Bridal Chamber

The Bridal Journey is a six-week online study which includes
Video Teaching
and
Worksheets
Based upon the keys and truths outlined in Bridal Redemption
Living Life Victoriously is not based upon our circumstances
It is determined by who we trust in the midst
of our circumstances
Join Us on the Journey
From Betrothal, to Preparation,
and into the Bridal Chamber
Begin Living as a Redeemed Bride
www.ElleUnlimited.com

35577747R00099

Made in the USA
Middletown, DE
07 October 2016